Owning Property Abroad
'Look Before You Leap'

*The practical guide to making
money from your dream holiday home*

by

Nathan Steel

**Grosvenor House
Publishing Limited**

This book is published by
Grosvenor House Publishing Ltd
28-30 High Street, Guildford, Surrey, GU1 3HY.
www.grosvenorhousepublishing.co.uk

A CIP record for this book
is available from the British Library

ISBN 978-1-906645-36-6

Contents

To our daughter,

*"The most beautiful and loving little
girl that we have ever seen, we love you
more than you will ever know sweetheart".*

Acknowledgments

Firstly, I want to say a huge 'Thank you' to my wife, who without her help, support and understanding over the years, it would have been virtually impossible for me to have achieved the things that I have.

I also want to thank my friend's Derek and John, who gave me the inspiration and self confidence to take the step into business and to whom I will always be grateful.

Introduction

It is the dream of many to become extremely wealthy yet the fortune of few. Many ideas to bring success, happiness and security have been thought of, some have been very successful indeed, yet the dreams of others have drifted, floundered and then disappeared without trace often leading to heartbreak and serious financial misery.

Some people find it difficult to come up with a rock solid, feasible and original idea which could lead to the success that so many yearn for. However, some find it easy to make someone else's idea work for them, when ironically it did not work for the person who thought of it in the first place.

There are countless questions to be asked about how to find the right highway to success and financial security and equally how to avoid the slippery slope to financial ruin. What is the secret of success? One may ask does this secret actually exist? And probably the biggest question of all for me - how do you achieve your goals in life and avoid failure?

This book is based upon my personal experience and illustrates my desire, personal drive and committed determination to seek out an idea which would provide an escape from the normal routine. You will see how such an ordinary person as myself, who had a very poor educational background and certainly had no knowledge of business management, created an alternative to a chosen career path and in the process changed my lifestyle, and that of my family, forever.

This incredible change was not only in real terms of actual wealth, but also in how to find those golden threads to success, which can lead any so-called 'very ordinary person' to pursue and capture their dream of a new start in life. When you absorb my words in the following chapters and combine my personal experiences with your dreams, it becomes clear that, like me, you can take control of your destiny and make decisions for yourself which will open many new doors in the future. You will also understand more about my journey as I describe my own personal thoughts, views and feelings and the many lessons learned during my progression towards the ultimate goal of completely changing my lifestyle. There are so many people out there who have the same desire and very similar goals or dreams.

This is my account as someone who had the passion and longing for change and financial success but used a very common idea to achieve it, the difference being that where countless others had failed, I succeeded.

There are no reasons whatsoever why you should not be as successful.

By using my research, practical knowledge, personal experiences and observations, this book will assist anyone who has had the urge or desire to buy property abroad. For those out there who have the intention of generating income from holiday property abroad, or who have in fact bought property, no matter where in the world and then found themselves disillusioned or in difficulties, these personal experiences may allow them to gain that invaluable information about how to make it work.

It will also explain how to generate additional income from other services and opportunities associated with property, and assist you along the road to success.

This balanced and realistic guide, which explains both the positive and more demanding challenges of property ownership abroad, will hopefully prevent your dreams from turning into a living financial nightmare.

When you examine the information contained within the following chapters, think of this in a very positive frame of mind. Think of it as guidance, based upon experience and an opportunity for you not to make the same mistakes as so many others have done who have travelled this well worn road.

As you take in this information and ponder on the personal experiences that are shared with you, it will become apparent that there is a certain sequence of events that are almost predictable. However, such events can only be seen and are only predictable through time and one's experience. A catch twenty two situation you may say, however, this guide will break that circle and provide you with the vision and foresight, which may assist you to make very informed decisions and help you to create your pathway to success.

Generally, this very clear and distinct sequence of events will lead to one of two outcomes. The first of these outcomes being personal satisfaction and the associated happiness that goes with it, in breaking out of the vicious circle of routine and securing that ambition of financial success. The other being disillusionment, frustration and unhappiness after being unable to generate income from your holiday home, false promises from others that have dashed your hopes, all of which will ultimately lead to financial problems and then failure to realise your dreams. The latter can also have an adverse effect on some in relation to their health and well being as the stress and deep regret of entering into such a situation can lead to sleepless nights and other associated problems as they see their dream, together with a considerable chunk of their money, disappearing down the pan.

You will be able to see how and why this sequence unfolds, and the experiences which are explained will greatly increase your opportunity of success and deflect you away from failure.

They say that hindsight is the perfect science, and this can certainly be argued in the case of carving out your way to success. As you travel along this pathway with me, let my personal experience help you to cut your journey time to achieving your goals and allow my experience to aid your vision. If you are going to enter into such a venture, go into it with your eyes wide open and with one clear intention. That intention should be one of 'I want to be successful, I am going to be successful and I know exactly how I am going to get there'.

Get it right before you even start !

This book represents what most people who are successful can relate too, and that is, if you want something desperately enough, you will work day in and day out to achieve it.

So what made this very basic and unoriginal idea so very successful for me and how could it work for you?

CHAPTER 1

That Yearn for Something More

As I drove from the office at Charing Cross, my thoughts started to wander. 4.10am on a cold, wet, windy morning in central London, the pavements almost deserted, old newspapers blowing about in the gutter and the odd homeless person trying to keep warm in a cardboard strewn doorway.

We made our way through the West End toward the hotel where the others in my team would be staying for a few days until the job was over. There I was, a lad from the north of England, scuttling through the streets of the capital at some unearthly time of the night, doing a job that some would describe as being for 'queen and country'. Somehow, I thought to myself, I had let almost twenty years slip through my fingers. I enjoyed my job, in fact I loved what I was doing. Even though I say it myself, I was an absolutely determined, hard working, totally reliable and dedicated professional, committed to achieving great results. I was a real team player, always giving 110% whatever I did, but one day it would be over and what would I have to show for it except a pension and some great stories and adventures to look back on. I had what could be described as an exciting job, in fact at times, a very exciting job. I was part of a close knit team who looked after each other when we did our weird, wonderful and often dangerous things, but I knew that things would eventually change and I wanted to prepare for a different future, which would bring along with it a new kind of excitement.

I needed something that I could do in my own time, away from the work environment which would assist in giving me some stability for once and provide a safe and better quality of life in the years to come. I could continue what I was doing for some years in the private sector if I needed to, and undoubtedly I could travel the world in that capacity. I knew that the opportunity was still there to experience that type of excitement, but I also knew that I wanted to feel a completely different kind of excitement.

In reality, it would be a business venture, which I could put as much or as little of my own time into as I wanted or that I could allow, and the measure of success would be gauged by the amount of additional income that I would generate. In short, making money would be my new excitement, which would replace the adventures and excitement of my 'ordinary' daytime job. I knew that my colleagues would see this as a very sedate change to my professional lifestyle, however, I could see the very strong possibilities that lay ahead.

Even though I had no experience in business whatsoever, I was aware of my own strengths. There was no doubt about my drive, absolute commitment and sheer determination. I knew that I had the willpower to achieve in whatever I did and I knew that I had an extremely positive frame of mind no matter what I was doing. I enjoyed a challenge or what some may describe as any character building situation, and I would always keep going. I was a 'down to earth' type of person who could communicate with people from all walks of life. I enjoyed talking and socialising with people and I knew that this was something that I could harness and use, in some way, in the future. I also knew, however, that there was one other ingredient missing that would keep me going through any difficult times that may come along and that, quite simply, was I needed to identify an incentive to achieve success.

Making money was that incentive. Making money may not appeal to everyone, but it certainly appealed to me !

John, a real good friend, trusted colleague and who could only be described as a totally dedicated professional, was sitting in the front passenger seat. He must have noticed that my thoughts were miles away from the wet dimly lit streets that we were travelling along. He asked me what I was thinking about and he probably thought that I was going to say something about the job that we were working on at the time. When I told him, there was a stunned silence followed by a request, in a somewhat expletive way, for me to "Say that again".

It could have been a mistake in talking about it until I had everything in place, but what the hell, I completely trusted John. "I'm going to buy property abroad. I want to totally change my lifestyle".

To some, this may not have sounded like a very exciting idea, but when compared to what I was doing for a living, that particular type of excitement would end at some time and I knew that I would need to fill that void in some other way. Although I had a considerable amount of job satisfaction, I also new that I would never get rich doing my daytime job. There were great possibilities for the future if I had something that I could call my own. Money could, and would, buy me a completely different kind of excitement.

There were some words that had stuck in my mind and which summed it up for me, and that was, "No matter what you do, you'll never get rich working for someone else".

Whether that's right or wrong, I personally, could see why it could be true. I did not like the idea of retiring from my daytime job and working hard for the rest of my life, just for someone else to reap the benefits, and become even wealthier, as a result of my hard labour, knowledge, contacts, personal experience, and professional qualifications or advice.

I also did not like the thought of someone, basically, telling me how much I was worth !

Due to the nature of my work, the other major factor in my personal drive was that I would still be relatively young when I retired, only 48, which, in my book, was certainly young !

I had thought about it for a while. Entering the international property world of 'buy to let' was certainly an absolute change in my career path. It was a small, basic, but manageable idea which had the potential to grow and generate what I thought would be a reasonable amount of income. More importantly, it was apparent that there were other ways of making a considerable amount of money which were attached to it and linked in perfectly with the renting out of holiday property. Put all that together and I knew that I was looking at seriously increasing my earning potential. Now that really did appeal and excite me !

Although I had obviously considered the possibility of growth, I could not have imagined at that time how important that consideration was going to be.

In the bigger scheme of things, to a person who was wealthy or financially comfortable, it would be no big deal to launch into such a venture as they would have sufficient finance available to keep the business afloat if things did not go to plan.

The only problem was that I was certainly not wealthy and if things did not work out then I could end up with serious financial problems.

However, on a more positive note, if I thought things through and produced a basic business plan so that I was fully aware of where I was going and how and when I was going to get there, I would reduce the risks considerably. Detailed planning and organising were two of my strengths and this was another good platform on which to build the other ingredients of such a business venture.

I knew in my own mind that the time was right to do something positive. If I did not do it now I would never do it and I would regret that for the rest of my life. It would be a risk, but a calculated one at that.

I looked at other very successful people in business. They must have had similar thoughts when they first started out and probably had taken much larger risks than this, but they must also have had the confidence in their own ability, personal drive, sheer determination and overall, a positive outlook. Was this the key to success?

To assist me on my way to being successful in this business venture, there were two sayings which I would refer to on many occasions when things became a little challenging.

The first was "There is no such thing as problems only solutions", a very common quote, granted, but none the less very important to me.

The second was "Never ever say that you cannot do something, instead turn it on its head and think - How can I achieve that?"

I had used the last quote many times over the years in my day time job when we had encountered problems or ran into more challenging situations.

Those few words would spur me on to focus the brain, to think positively and hunt out the way to success instead of closing down the positive thought processes. I was well aware that success and wealth were rarely handed out on a plate, but I also knew that I had the determination to work hard for it and achieve my dreams.

The idea was in place, now the work had to start.

CHAPTER 2

Researching the idea

What you are about to read is relevant to anywhere at all in the world, wherever you may be considering buying your dream holiday home, or in fact, where you may actually own property at this time.

The general principles are arguably the same, whether it is in America, Europe, Asia or further afar. Relate these experiences to any country or location that you may be considering buying property to rent out with a view to generating income, and fit what you read around your idea.

Remember, and I can not stress this enough, it is the principles of what you will see unfold, which is based upon actual experience, that is the important factor.

My personal experiences lay over 4,000 miles away, in the United States of America.

America was a country that I had never set foot in, never mind bought property. Some may say it is the land of opportunity, but for me, at that time, the jury was still most definitely out. The one thing that I did know was that it certainly had the potential to be a very good opportunity indeed for me, providing that I did my research and I was thorough in how I carried out that research.

I knew that I had a very feasible idea and that I was not the first person by far to think of doing such a thing. But where would I start in this vast area of research to ensure that my dream of success would be achieved.

I was very much aware that a lot of people who had tried renting out holiday property in the state of Florida, and other places in the world for that matter, had become disillusioned, failed and as a result suffered serious financial misery. I needed to know exactly what they had done and how they had gone so drastically wrong.

Failure for me was simply not an option and I knew that there must be some way of navigating away from failure and achieving my goals.

I started by reading books, reports and sifting through mounds of market research about Florida produced by various travel organisations both in the United Kingdom and the United States of America. These included documents, maps and brochures compiled by high street travel agents, airline companies, television holiday programmes, newspapers and travel magazines. I took specific interest in reports from tourist information offices especially in relation to visitor attractions such as the major theme parks and sites or locations of special interest, where tourists would certainly want to visit.

I contacted and spoke with a number of villa owners who were doing something similar but the feedback that I was receiving ranged from "Don't do it – it's a costly nightmare" to "Well you might cover your costs, but you'll be lucky". Overall, it was a fairly negative type of response, but surely, it could not all be as bad as some made out.

I did not just want to be lucky, I wanted to plan this business venture correctly from the start. I needed to have solid foundations in place where my business could grow and not build upon sand where, without the correct advice, research, knowledge and contingency plans, the business would collapse into financial oblivion

After listening to various villa owners I was not satisfied with the doom and gloom aspect. I kept on saying to myself – THINK POSITIVE !

I have always been an extremely positive person, even when I have found myself in difficult, very demanding and what some might call extremely stressful situations. By assessing the situation, thinking clearly when under pressure, developing a strategy, identifying options, applying a common sense approach and a positive thought process, I have always come through in the end. That, I knew, was due to years of training in my day time job. That training had moulded me and provided a frame work which had never let either me or my team down. I had always been calm in crisis and decisive during times of action.

The three questions that I needed answering immediately were firstly, was it true what some property owners were saying? Secondly, were they telling me this because I would be in competition with them? and thirdly, if it was as bad as they made out, what were these people doing wrong?

I wanted and needed to know more.

I knew that droves of people, not just in their hundreds of thousands, but in their millions, visited Florida each year and they all had something in common. That common factor was, no matter from where they came, they all spent money to get there and once they arrived in Florida, they spent even more.

You can now see the picture building up and this may be relevant to many other locations in the world, wherever you may be considering buying, or indeed, where you may have already actually purchased your property.

I needed to find a way of harnessing some of this visitor spending power and direct it toward my venture and ultimately, into my pocket !

At this point, I want to make it quite clear that, by no means, can I be described as being an arrogant person. I would also like to make it very clear indeed that I make no apology whatsoever, for sounding like I was being driven by making money. The truth of the matter is that was exactly what was driving me so hard.

As my research confirmed, Florida commonly known as 'The Sunshine State' was arguably the biggest family tourist destination in the world.

My comparisons with other holiday destinations around the globe had totally confirmed that Florida was the right choice for me to locate my property. There were many overriding factors why it had to be Florida. This had soon become apparent during my research, but the basic principals of operating such a business would have been similar wherever I had decided to locate, whether it had been France, Spain, Portugal, Cyprus or the Canary Islands for example.

Florida had everything in its favour, such as a reputation for good weather, day in - day out and all year around. It also had very easy accessibility on a daily basis to and from major International Airports from all around the world. Florida, as a result of a very good exchange rate at the time, was great value for money. It was renowned for its theme parks, fun rides and attractions, designed for both children and adults, which were constantly growing in size with new, bigger and better ideas which, in my eyes, were second to none. My research revealed that there were vast areas of land owned by the worldwide renowned theme parks such as Walt Disney World and Universal Studios that were yet undeveloped, but when those sites were extended and new parks created this would not only bring in new tourists to the area, it would also ensure that people who had been to Central Florida would want to return to explore the new and even more futuristic attractions.

Florida had so much to offer. Putting the theme parks to one side, there was so much more to be seen in this fantastic part of America. It has a fabulous coastline, breathtaking sun drenched beaches and some of the most beautiful wildlife in their natural environment to be seen anywhere in the world. Combine all of those factors and you can see why I was initially attracted to Florida.

This, to me at that time, were some of the clearest indications that pointed to the fact that the long term tourist demand for holiday accommodation would always be on the increase in that part of the world.

With somewhere in the region of forty million visitors in 2000 for example, and in my view, that number would certainly increase in future years, Florida, especially Central Florida, had the right assets for my business plan to succeed.

It was soon very apparent that, generally, UK visitors on holiday in Central Florida usually resided in one of three types of accommodation i.e. hotels, motels or private holiday villas. This point alone threw up a number of questions, the obvious one to me being, how many families stayed in a hotel or motel on their first visit to Florida and realised their mistake of having to share a small hotel room, with very limited facilities and no privacy, for two or even three weeks?

If it were a package holiday, where for example, the customer was staying in a hotel on a theme park, they probably would have been shepherded onto buses at the airport and then driven to the resort or complex, and the chances were that they would not have a hire vehicle to explore the vast areas of Florida. They would in effect be limited to the confines of the hotel and theme park for the duration of their stay unless they travelled by taxi or hired a vehicle, that is, if they remembered to take their driving licence with them. By that time, they had arrived in Florida and that would be an unforeseen expense and a costly mistake at that.

That area of research was of great interest to me. I knew that all I had to do was divert sufficient numbers of people away from the hotels and motels and into my own private holiday accommodation and fill up my 'calendar of availability' for the maximum amount of weeks in the year. Providing I charged the right price to guests, which would be both attractive and competitive against the high street travel agents package deals, whilst covering my overheads, the business would be a success. Sounds easy, but would it be?

This simple train of thought indicated that I could at least break even on my investment and that I would not have to put my hand into my own pocket to pay for the costs of buying and operating the property. However, I was not satisfied with that. If I was going to do this I would do it to generate maximum profit in order that it would have a significant effect to change my lifestyle in the future.

My view from the start was why break even when you can make a profit?

I never lost sight of the thought and belief that this venture had to be a life changing experience for me. It may be sufficient for some people that to cover their costs is all that they require, but why stop there when you could make a huge financial impact for the better on your future. Why go only half way when you can go all the way? I knew people, and very intelligent people at that, who would often say "I don't want to be rich". I used to think to myself, did those people actually realise what they were saying and if so, did they mean it?

Were they really happy with their lot, or could they just not see the vicious circle that they were in, which in essence was a cycle of working just to have a basic standard of living or survival in some cases, and essentially, to pay the bills?

Whenever I heard comments such as that, I kept visualising a hamster in a cage running on its exercise wheel. The hamster probably did that every day as part of its daily routine, and one thing that was certain, it was going absolutely nowhere fast !

I also believed that although some people liked the idea of being wealthy, they either could not be bothered to work for it, or they would make excuses for themselves as to why they could not do it or let others do the work for them and hope that they would reap the benefits from others around them. I also lost count of the number of people who said that they could do what I was doing if they wanted to, but they chose not to for a myriad of reasons - Oh really !

I made a comparison between those people and people who worked for themselves and who were successful in business. I soon realised that in relation to their outlook, mindset, rationale, personal drive and determination, there was no comparison at all ! I had no doubt that those who were in business, working for themselves, had a completely different mindset altogether.

I scrutinised what some people were saying and what I took as their somewhat narrow views, and it did actually give me inspiration. Some had actually laughed and really tried to knock what I was doing. The effect of that type of attitude was that it made me even more determined to succeed.

Generally, those who laughed or tried to mock me in some way, were so wrapped up in their daytime jobs working for large organisations that they could not see that there was a whole new world outside of their totally blinkered lifestyle.

This, however, was about me and my family future now and as far as I was concerned, that was what counted and not them.

There was one major question that had to be answered in relation to owning property abroad and one which everyone should seriously and closely examine before they commit themselves to such a venture.

That question was "Will I be able to get a sufficient number of guest bookings placed into the property to at least cover my costs and if I can not achieve that in the early stages will I have sufficient resources to cover the monthly expenses of such a venture and maintain my lifestyle as it is now?

Initially, that was the million dollar question and the enormity of that question is as significant now for anyone thinking of buying their own property abroad as it was to me many years ago.

For someone just starting out, this was and as I have clearly outlined, still is, the whole crux of the matter. Without the bookings, things would soon go drastically wrong and the property would soon become a severe drain on resources.

After speaking with many property owners, I am convinced that this very basic question had not been fully probed and answered by many people who had entered into such a venture, and so many had been taken by that 'warm and fuzzy feeling' of the moment.

You may think, at this point, who is he to tell me this, insulting people's intelligence like that. Please do not be offended. I do not intend to insult or offend in any way. However, I certainly do intend to provide you with as much information as possible, without any gloss or spin, which will allow you to make very informed decisions, before you commit yourself. I am a total realist and I am purely relaying to you some of the experiences that I have encountered over many years in this particular field.

Please remember, there are people who own property abroad, and there are people who successfully own and operate property business abroad.

I kept thinking back to all of those people who said that they did not want to be rich and I could not get their comments, views and rationale out of my mind. The reason that I could not forget them was simply due to the fact that those were the very people who, in the long term, would probably come to me to rent my holiday property or purchase a product from me, and therefore, put their money into my pocket. Who would be laughing then? As my business developed, that's certainly what happened in a number of cases and I did laugh to myself after saying thank you to them when they gave me their money.

As I have mentioned earlier, it would appear that many people do get caught up in what I can only describe as this 'warm and fuzzy feeling' of the moment. A brief example of one such moment came to light when I was contacted by someone who had taken a holiday in a certain part of the world, again renowned for its tourist industry. On the last day of his holiday, he said that he had seen a new development that was still under construction. He had gone into the development, chosen a plot of land and a style of house that he liked, and which was illustrated on some plans, and then signed the agreement. He paid an initial deposit for the new build, left and returned to the UK.

What was the result, you may well ask?

A little bit of a shock when he returned, you might say ! Apparently, it was certainly not what he expected.

Briefly, he described how the house was a lot smaller than he had imagined, it had a private 'swimming pool', which apparently was more like a large bath tub and the house was miles and miles away from the main tourist area that attracted most of the tourist rental trade. Generally, I have found that tourists, especially those with children want to be near the busier areas and do not want to travel miles upon miles to get there and back. It was just too far away and that was the first signs of problems... location, location, location!

What made him do such a thing? I am totally convinced that he is not alone and many other people have made very similar, spur of the moment decisions.

Was it as a result of a combination of things, such as the feel good factor, after being on a wonderful holiday and seeing bustling new property developments, or returning home and seeing television programmes and glossy magazines showing fabulous apartments and houses, which tell people how much they can make in rental and re-sale value.

The whole aspect of renting out property is made to sound so easy and is generally skimmed over.

Just stop and ask yourself, in reality, how easy is it to attract paying guests to a holiday property?

For most people, owning property abroad is probably a dream and a life long ambition, and for a vast majority of property owners, renting out the property is the very heartbeat of those dreams. Without securing the essential guest bookings would certainly mean serious financial problems ahead. I will go into considerable detail later in relation to how to attract guests to your home and, basically, hopefully assist to turn your dreams into hard cash, and ultimately, happiness and security.

When people do such a spontaneous or impulsive thing, it may have been the result of listening to a good sales pitch by property salespeople, seeing well put together videos of blue sky, golden sanded beaches and beautifully inviting clear sea with sunshine beating down on nearby new developments or resorts. It may also be those factors combined with the 'reassurance' of what can be described as somewhat questionable promises from some who say that they will place bookings in your property on your behalf which would cover your costs, but were actually bookings which failed to materialise. If you hear the word 'guarantee' when it comes to someone else placing bookings into your property, my view is, run a mile ! In this day and age, it is arguable to say that no-one can guarantee anything.

Reliance upon a third party was just not part of my plans. Assistance maybe, reliance, definitely not !

Was that why so many property owners had suffered serious financial problems in the past? Was this why so many people had failed to become successful in something which had such great potential?

Once again, this critical area of marketing will be fully explored later.

As I delved further into my research other questions were being thrown up which definitely required answers. For example, what type of property would be the most suitable and desirable to rent out? Ideally, where should it be located? Who should I speak with to get the best advice on buying such a property? How and where would I get a mortgage? What about banking, exchange rates and what taxes would I have to pay? Ultimately, what about re-sale value? The list of questions grew steadily.

This seemed to be getting complicated so I decided to break it down and deal with it stage by stage, the result being that the answers emerged from the mist and things became much clearer and easier to understand. It also ensured that I covered all of the ground and gleaned as much information as possible to assist in my decision making process.

Speaking of mist there was something else which I needed to find out more about and that was the weather. We all know that Florida is called "The Sunshine State", but like many others I had heard stories about hurricanes and tornados. What would happen, apart from the obvious damage and destruction of course, if I bought property and it was hit by a tornado for example?

It was apparent that Florida did suffer to a certain degree from such storms and weather problems, however, after reading various articles, reports and books I became satisfied with my findings. In the bigger scheme of things if the weather in Florida was so bad would billions of dollars have been invested in organisations such as Walt Disney World, Universal Studios, the vast array of other companies, theme parks and attractions and even NASA at Kennedy Space Center.

I was re-assured in this respect and I will later explain about something called Hazard Insurance to cover your property against such rare events.

As a side issue I also soon found that the locals in Florida are obsessed with weather forecasts. They also have a very good system to warn of storms and, for example, had actually predicted that in one particular year, for the period of June through to November they were expecting 9 Tropical Storms and 5 major Hurricanes. According to their weather channel on television this does not mean they are going to hit Florida, they are in the vicinity of Florida which, may I say, is a vast area.

Another re-assuring fact is that one of the ideal locations for holiday rental property is in central Florida where most of the major theme parks are located, away from the coast, where some of the storms may hit. Without going into all of the details, it was also apparent that, generally, if a bad storm, a hurricane for example, did hit the area of Florida, by the time it hit land-fall, the energy within it started to dissipate and by the time the weather front hit central Florida its was no where near as powerful or as problematic.

After months of research, I had made my mind up to buy property, and for me it would be in Florida.

At this juncture, I would like to remind you not to lose sight of the general principals that I am relaying to you, as your dreams may lie in some other part of the world. Keep your vision and personal preferences firmly at the forefront of your mind, and fit your circumstances around the experiences which will be outlined.

All that you need to remember is that if what I did worked for me, then why should it not work for you?

CHAPTER 3

Taking the big step

Now that I was satisfied that I had a good business plan and my research into the feasibility of the whole venture had been as thorough as possible, my decision was made. Although quite daunting, it was a strangely exciting decision to make and I was ready to take that big step. But just how was I going to do it?

At this point, I should clearly inform you that I am not a financial advisor in any way, shape, form or description and what I am about to share with you is only the way that I started my business. Other people may do it in a different way but that is an individual choice or decision.

I will keep this brief, but highlight the very important and relevant aspects and endeavour to point out some of the pitfalls and areas of concern that I identified. You may find this to be of great benefit and this may act as a steer to anyone who may be about to purchase property in Florida or anywhere else for that matter, or who already own property, but are encountering problems or difficulties.

It was obvious that to purchase a property I needed to have a certain amount of money available. My research revealed that, at the time, I could obtain a mortgage in America for up to 80% of the price of the property, secured against the house in America and therefore if I went down this road I would need to find a deposit of 20%, which was the minimum deposit that would be accepted. This meant that if for any reason the business did not work out and I ended up being unable to pay the mortgage, the lender or title company, would foreclose on the property and it would not effect me in England, except that I would lose the property in Florida, and my initial investment. That would, of course, have had a knock on effect with any customers that had booked to stay in the villa who would be extremely disappointed to say the least and that was something that I did not want, or could allow to happen, under any circumstances.

Alternatively, I could use savings that I had and also obtain a loan in the United Kingdom but that would have been secured against my home in England.

After looking at various options I decided two things. The first was that in no way would I risk losing my home in England. I knew that some risks were worth taking and others were not. The second, as mentioned earlier, was that failure was simply not an option. From the start I was going to show complete commitment and throw myself right into this venture to ensure that it did work.

A very important decision that I took at that time was that whatever happened I would keep my personal and business life totally separate.

As I only had limited resources I was only prepared to invest a certain amount into the business. The question was, how would I free up sufficient funds to invest into the business to get it up and running, whilst protecting and keeping the remainder secure as a safety net.

I looked closely at two things :-

1. What was in my 'Asset Column' which I should keep safe and untouched?
2. What was in my 'liability Column', which I should use to assist financing the business?

My asset column consisted of anything that would or could make me money, for example, property which in fact was my home, any stocks and shares and investment saving schemes through my place of work which, when they matured, would provide considerable lump sums.

My liability column consisted of anything else which was of value at the time but would depreciate in overall value in a fairly short space of time. The best and most obvious example of a liability was my car.

That, for me, was the answer. At the time I owned a BMW, an ex-demonstrator from a local BMW dealership. It was only just over 8 months old and it was still worth a considerable amount of money. I had owned relatively new, good class motor cars for some years but my view now was that, yes, they were lovely cars to drive around in but would they make me any money?

The answer was a resounding no, they certainly would not. They were, at that time in my life, a definite financial liability and that liability had to be turned into an asset. My thoughts from the very beginning were positive and therefore, I knew that there would be plenty of time for new cars in the future, when I became successful in business.

In the mean time, I needed to release some funds to finance my deposit on a property in Florida and if it meant driving around in an old car well so be it – it would not be the end of the world – only the start of my new world. The property in Florida would then become a definite asset. The decision was therefore made. The BMW had to go. It was a shock, but I would get over it.

I immediately advertised the vehicle for sale. I was aware that the sale price of the BMW would be there or thereabouts to make up the 20% deposit on the property in my price bracket, but I had to concede that I would have to use a very small amount of savings to make up the difference. That I was prepared to do and the words speculate to accumulate sprung to mind !

At this stage I knew that I could raise the 20% deposit for the property but what else would I have to do and what else would I need to understand about purchasing a property abroad.

I needed to know what other costs would be involved in buying and operating property in Florida. If I were to obtain a mortgage in America there were bound to be fees involved or commissions being paid to someone, somewhere along the line.

Would there be attorney fee's, search fee's and many other fee's and taxes associated with buying property. All of these would be taking money out of my pocket.

If you are considering buying property in Florida for example, I have found that the easiest way of describing what you will expect to pay is to try and obtain a copy of a form known as a 'HUD 1 Settlement Statement', which is issued by the U.S. Department of Housing and Urban Development.

Briefly, this will give a summary of borrower's transactions and a summary of seller's transactions. Basically you will be able to see what you will have to pay, and with a little research, why you are required to pay it. There may be similar type forms for other locations in the world, and it may be a good starting point to find out at a very early stage to prevent any unexpected financial surprises.

Some areas itemised on the form can be a little confusing and you would be very wise to clarify exactly what they mean and why it is included. For example, there are various processing, insurance, recording, assessment, taxes and stamp fees outlined, and you really do need to know how much they will cost you. If you can find a friendly and helpful property owner that has been through the whole process and has property located in the same area that you are considering buying in, then it may be very beneficial to speak or meet with them, if at all possible.

One important area to fully understand is if you deal with a mortgage broker ask him or her what companies, if any, are they tied to recommend and what commissions will they receive. These commissions will be itemised on the 'HUD 1' form, and when you look closely you may see that the mortgage broker could receive a considerable fee indeed, which could run into thousands of dollars.

Ask yourself - is it the best advice for you as an individual or is it the best advice for the broker to receive their commission and just as importantly who will pay the commission at the end of the day – the lending company or you the property purchaser?

Also look very closely at the level of interest that you will be paying back on your loan. This can be considerably higher than you may first think. As I write the level of interest in the U.K. stands around the 5% mark but I have spoken with people who have or who are purchasing property in Florida at the moment, and are paying way above that figure. Take that figure over a period of a 30 year mortgage, which seems to be the norm for a vast amount of foreign nationals who purchase holiday property in Florida, and you are now looking at a seriously high pay back figure.

If you have obtained details about securing a mortgage via a mortgage broker for example, it may well be a good idea to make a comparison with banks who can offer the same or a very similar service or product to that of a mortgage broker but you may find that it could be a much easier and a considerably less expensive way of obtaining your loan. Once again, pay close attention not just to the rate of interest that you will be paying but also to any fee's, commissions or tie in clauses that may also be included somewhere in the small print.

It really is essential to closely examine all of these little extras, which are sometimes hidden away in the vast array of documents and papers that you may be presented with, and this again will apply to any country or location, and not just Florida. It may be stating the obvious, but be wary of any sales pitch that you may be given in an effort to secure your signature, don't be hurried and take as much time as you need to read and understand all of the documentation. I cannot emphasise enough, check and question the fees and rates that are itemised as they will have to be paid somewhere along the line and normally, in America, at a time they call 'Closing'.

You may think that I am stating the obvious, but I am aware of people who have not fully read or understood what has been said or written and it has been a costly mistake for them indeed. I have lost count of the number of people with whom I have spoken, who own holiday villas or apartments all over the world, and they have been hit by unexpected expense when it came to the time of closing or actually taking possession of the property. This unexpected expense could and should have been identified much earlier in the process of buying property, and I must ask myself, is that the fault of the potential buyers for missing or misunderstanding the detail or small print, or did the fault lie with those selling the property for not fully explaining everything to the buyers. Maybe, the answer lies somewhere in between !

In relation to America, 'Closing' is similar to exchanging contracts and that's when a large chunk of your money will leave your hands and the property will be signed over to you. During this signing over procedure, a notary will be present. A notary is a person who can witness signatures on legal or binding documents. Once again a fee will be charged for this service. I will mention the experiences of 'closing', a little later, which you may find, from a very practical point of view, very useful indeed.

You can now see that the cost of buying the property is starting to rise. You need to be fully aware of these extra expenses. It will appear that everything you do or everything that needs to be done to purchase the property has a fee or cost attached to it somewhere, and that is just about right.

Although all of the process can be completed without an attorney, it may be wise to seek advice before you commit yourself. If there is a language barrier involved, you may well consider this to be essential.

I was now at the stage where I had completed my research into the feasibility of the idea, I new that I wanted to go ahead with my plan, I had some idea about mortgages and how much I could afford to borrow to buy a property and I had a good idea about additional related costs. The next step would be the actual procedure in relation to applying for a mortgage. Baring in mind that I was a foreign national, what would I have to show to qualify for a mortgage in America?

Again, please remember to relate these very relevant experiences into the area of research, and to the country, where you are considering your property purchase.

In my circumstances, that of a foreign national applying for a mortgage in Florida, it was necessary to show proof of my identity, employment and earnings in the U.K. It was necessary for me to show that, if I had a mortgage in the U.K., that no arrears were outstanding. My previous six months pay advice slips were also required as well as any proof of investments i.e. savings schemes, stocks and shares, bonds etc. This was all to show that I was a 'sound' financial risk to the lender.

Florida has had quite a stringent process for many years in relation to foreign nationals buying property. One of the reasons for this, as I understand it, was to ensure that property was not being bought up through money laundering scams, as a result of illegal drug trafficking. It is well known that, due to the geographic location of Florida in relation to some of the main illegal drug producing areas of the world, that the seedy world of drug trafficking had a huge financial impact in the 'Sunshine State'. It has to be said that, although the abhorrent illicit trade of drug trafficking via Florida was, and arguably still is a problem, it has not affected the tourist industry in any way that I am aware of. It was, and still is, something that can and does happen in many other countries around the world, but is not obvious to the ordinary, decent person on holiday. This did not effect or concern me or my overall business plan at all.

In addition, as a result of the horrific events of September 11, 2001, the Homeland Security Act ensured that all procedures, systems and processes were scrutinised and again tightened up. This was particularly relevant to foreign nationals entering the United States of America, for whatever reason, be it as a tourist or on business, which included actually buying property. I will mention the effects that 9/11 had on me and many others, later.

What would I have to do now? I had visited the usual property exhibitions and spoken with numerous people from various companies. The representatives from those companies said all the right things, the things that people wanted to hear. All were extremely positive and very enthusiastic, that was obvious from their sales pitch.

The problem that I had with this was that there were very few negative things forthcoming during those conversations. I had been shown very professionally compiled videos of developments in Central Florida, and some European countries for that matter, with fantastic golf courses and great facilities, which were topped off with scenes covering everything from arriving at the airport to visiting all the major theme parks and attractions. I had listened to well prepared presentations about the magical feeling of owning your very own property which would also have its very own swimming pool. It really did look out of this world. I asked for and had been provided with various documents and assorted pieces of literature, including bundles of glossy magazines of up and coming developments from the companies involved in the promotions and exhibitions. The literature included site plans, floor plans and price lists of the various show houses, or models, as they are known in America and I must say on the face of it I had to say that it did look very tempting indeed. The task for me now was to remove that gloss and get into the bones of the sales staff and find out how things really were.

After listening to the sales pitch from the representatives I must have had what seemed like a million questions to ask them. I had heard the positive side of things but what about the drawbacks and why had so many people, who had bought this type of property in the past and attempted this type of venture, gone so seriously wrong.

It was apparent that, generally, the salespeople that I had spoken with were trying to sell two things. The first was actual real estate and the second was property management services. After all, someone had to look after your property when you live so far away.

It was obvious that the staff were employed to sell these two services to people like myself, however, was this similar in principle to the mortgage brokers or consultants? If they were selling to me who was paying them? Was it their employers on a commission basis and if so, where would that commission come from, or was it, unknowingly at this time, somehow going to be me at the end of the day?

I asked these people more questions, delved and probed this area, but the answers from some on this subject were slow in coming back. The more that I questioned them about it, the more uncomfortable I became. To cut a long story short, I eventually found out that salespeople, including the American equivalent of estate agents, called realtors, could make very considerable commissions indeed on property sales. It also became clear that their most lucrative commissions came mainly from the sale of new properties and there were various ways in which commissions could be paid. Normally, the commissions were included in the price of a new house and paid by the builder as a percentage of the total cost of the property that was sold. This, in reality, came to many thousands of dollars for each house that they sold. The more they sold the more money they earned. The larger the house and lot size to build it upon, the larger the cost involved, and therefore, the larger the commission that could be available. So by persuading people to add on little extra's to their new property, such as having an additional bathroom fitted, increasing the size of the pool deck area and swimming pool or having expensive floor tiles laid etc. etc, could give the salesperson an even larger pay-packet.

Was this the main reason why everything that I was being told was unbelievably positive?

At this point, I metaphorically ran to my locker of quotes and sayings and brought out another one, which was "If something sounds too good to be true – then it probably is ".

I still needed to know why so many people had failed in the past. I asked the sales staff about the property management aspect of business and, once again, the way it was described to me by them sounded too good to be true. My own personal thought was that everything in the garden was too rosy for my liking. Could it be that this area was one of the main reasons why people had found themselves in financial dire straits and could it be a very lucrative source of income for property management companies? I then decided to make my own enquiries into property management. I will go on to explain my 'eye opening findings' later, and this is a subject that you should really take in if you want to keep your money in your pocket.

I had heard a lot about buying new properties but I decided to cover all of the bases and therefore I researched older second hand property, known as 'Resale's', as well. Would there be any benefits in buying an older resale property?

To get a good look at what was on offer in the used property market I obtained dozens of copies of American estate agent or real estate magazines, newspapers and brochures. It was then that I decided to upgrade my home computer, and buy a relatively decent one with a software package that would be useful for my business. Although I have not gone into it in any depth at all, and I must add that I had very limited computer skills at that time, the internet was certainly useful in my research, and it would later be the most essential tool in my new business. You will see how it literally did open the doorway to the world for me and how it generated a large amount of my new financial income.

I now had a good balanced view of the property markets from which I could at least make an informed decision on the right way forward.

CHAPTER 4

Buying the perfect holiday rental property

I had now made considerable progress toward turning an idea into something tangible. The big question now was what type of property should I purchase?

I asked myself a vast amount of questions and formulated the answers on two different levels, based upon research and personal holiday experience. The first level being in the eyes of a person who in fact would be a paying customer, and the second level, as the actual property owner.

What would I require as an owner and very importantly, what were the needs of holiday makers who, after all, were the people who would either make me or break me.

One of the first things that I had found was that, generally, land in Florida was subject to zones and there were basically three types of zones. The first type being zoned for residential properties, the second being zoned for short term rental properties and the third type of zone was designated for commercial properties.

In order for me to undertake the business as I had planned, I would be restricted by regulations and therefore I would have to buy a property which was located in a short term rental zone.

Briefly, as the title suggests a 'Residential Zone' is for exactly that. It is a zone which incorporates residential properties.

A 'Short Term Rental Zone' is a designated area, on which the properties that are built are licensed to be subject of a short term rental agreement.

The term Short Term Rental means, that at the time of writing, property can be rented out by the owner and, generally, the only stipulation is that any person who rents the property can only do so for a maximum period of time. The period of time is normally measured in days as opposed to months. I found that, at the time, around 30 days was the maximum amount of time most counties would allow people to stay in short term rental accommodation. (Some states, counties or districts may vary). This did not present a problem, as generally, people on holiday were only likely to rent the property for a period of one, two or three weeks at a time. The duration of time being governed by the simple fact that they only had a limited number of days available for a holiday in any one year, and a major factor in that, for example, being work commitments.

My research found that there was an exception to that general rule. When I had first thought of ideas as to how I should market such property, I initially thought of three levels to direct my efforts. The first was locally, the second being nationally and last, but certainly not least, was the world wide market that was just waiting to be tapped into. It was at that point that I found that this general rule of short term rental was slightly different, mainly on the Gulf Coast area of Florida. Research showed that during the months of January, February and March, many Canadians travelled down from Canada to Florida to escape the bad weather at home and enjoy the lovely warm climate of the Sunshine State.

These Canadians, known as the Snow Birds, were quite a lucrative source of income for some, as they would stay in private accommodation for up to two or even three months at a time.

The other important factor was that, so many of these Snow Birds were creatures of habit, and they would re-book the same property for the following year.

Marketing is a huge subject in itself and you will see a little later some of the finer pointers towards how to achieve success in that most critical of areas.

Finally, the areas zoned 'Commercial' were, once again as suggested, for commercial properties only.

I also found that some zones had a mixture of residential and short term rental properties on the same estate or development. There were some benefits in buying a short term rental property in such an area. For example, it could mean that you may possibly have neighbours who would keep a watching eye on your property when you were not there. The drawback for the neighbours of course was the fact that every two or three weeks there would be a new set of holiday makers moving in next door and those on holiday would of course want to enjoy themselves and some may not be as considerate as others. Would this attract possible complaints from my Floridian neighbours, about the behaviour of any problematic guests? I could do without any such complaints or problematic guests for that matter.

I then took a close look at the various areas zoned for Short Term Rental property and tried to establish what exactly would make any one area stand out against another.

A number of factors would need to be considered in order to identify what I would consider to be the right Short Term Rental location. Although this would be a purely personal view, I started by thinking as a customer. What did I like and dislike about my accommodation and associated arrangements when I travelled abroad on holiday?

My list grew in no time at all and included the essential things such as it would have to be good, clean, spacious accommodation in a good safe desirable area. The area would need to be within a reasonable distance from the airport, but not so close that it would suffer from the noise of aircraft which would either be arriving or taking off.

The property would need to be close to all the local amenities and attractions including, for example, the main theme parks and visitor attractions, shops, restaurants, designer and factory retail outlets and the vast array of other areas of interest that tourists flock to see in Florida. I also liked to swim and play sport such as tennis and volleyball so the ideal place for me as a tourist would incorporate all of the above features.

But what about in the eyes of me, the actual property owner?

It may differ for properties in Spain, Portugal, France, Cyprus or the Canary Islands for example, however, I was satisfied that the desired property specifically for the Florida market, would need to fit into all of the above categories. In addition, I would need to know that the property was going to be as secure as possible for both the guests and for my peace of mind. The property should therefore be in an area which would be well illuminated, populated and near too, but not right on the side of a road, main thoroughfare or highway. The noise of passing traffic would be a major problem to guests. The area itself should be well maintained and generally give an immediate impression that the property is in the middle of a good and very desirable area. This in itself raised questions.

How can you ensure that not just your property but those around you are continuously well maintained and how would it effect your business if the house next door to you was left to wreck and ruin? Essentially, if you found yourself in that position, what could you actually do about it?

This took me back to an earlier question, and that being, should I consider buying a resale property?

During my research I took an in depth look at the resale property market. Initially that type of property looked an attractive proposition, for two main reasons. The first was that, on face value, prices and associated expenses appeared to be much lower than those properties on new developments and were generally well within my budget. Secondly, which was almost like a psychological safety net, and in reality, very false and misleading, if I bought a resale property it would be easier to start off and manage as my initial financial outlay and start up costs would not be as much compared to buying a new property.

After examining the finer points and thinking about things logically and rationally I came to the conclusion that in my view if I started off by purchasing a resale property, it would definitely be a bad move financially, and it would be a half hearted start into the business.

Some may think that it would be a good idea to test the water first, however, the rationale behind my thoughts and views had been confirmed time and time again when I spoke with owners who had purchased resale properties and whom had attempted such a business venture.

In my view, the common theme in such circumstances can be outlined in two words – False Economy.

This is borne out when discussing the pro's and cons of buying new or resale property. It may have seemed like a good idea to buy a resale and keep the initial financial outlay down to a minimum, but a number of things should be taken into consideration before taking the plunge into such a purchase.

Starting with the basics of maintaining the property, depending upon its age, compare that with a property of equal age at home. How do they compare and what problems would you expect to encounter? Then add the fact if this has been a short term rental property for some years, how many people have been through the front door and lived in the property over that period of time. All of these people will probably have been short term guests, mostly on holiday. How will they have treated the property when they were there? No doubt many people are very responsible and considerate and would have taken good care of things. Generally, they will have shown some respect for property which belong to others, unfortunately some people do not.

Some of the common problems that you may inherit after taking possession of an older property may range from the small irritable things to more major and potentially costly problems. Domestic appliance failure, such as cookers or microwaves breaking down, dishwashers or tumble dryers developing a leak, showers malfunctioning etc. are to be expected after a certain length of time.

However, structural problems and issues such as dampness appearing in the bathrooms or the untimely breakdown of an air conditioning unit or swimming pool heater are particularly unwelcome and undesirable.

I accept that some of these problems could occur in a new property, however, the chances that they will occur in an older property soon after you take over and when you are least prepared to deal with it both financially or logistically, are arguably greater.

Problems similar to those mentioned may seem very small in the bigger scheme of things. However, consider that you are at home thousands of miles away when something similar to this goes wrong, with an added twist that you may have guests either staying at the property right now or arriving shortly. What are you going to do?

Apart from the frustration that it may cause to you or your guests and depending on the scale of the problem that has occurred, who will be available to solve the problem for you and how quickly can it be resolved?

The other very important question is 'How much is it going to cost you to have the repairs carried out to a satisfactory standard?

If, for example, you have just recently purchased this resale property, it's already been an expensive time for you with the general start up costs and all of a sudden the air conditioning unit breaks down. If it is in the high season and baking hot outside, life for your guests without air conditioning is going to be unpleasant, uncomfortable and very sticky indeed. You're going to need that unit repaired as soon as possible. A breakdown such as this is going to be costly and an added expense that you just do not need, and did not expect, particularly when your resources may be a little low.

I again accept that this could occur in a new property, but the difference is that things such as structural repairs, air conditioning units, swimming pool heaters, fridge/freezers, microwave cookers, dishwashers, televisions, clothes washers and dryers etc. are all generally covered by a warranty for at least the first twelve months in a new property. You may also have the option of an extended warranty beyond that time. In an older property the chances of any warranty being in existence must be relatively low.So who would you call if such a problem occurs?

Unless you have arranged someone other than a management company to take care of and maintain your property, the first call that you probably are going to have to make is to either that person or your management company whichever is applicable.

The next thing to be ascertained is, if you have a new property which still has warranties in existence, the management company or the person elected by you to look after the property should get in touch with the building contractor on your behalf to firstly see if the warranty covers that particular fault or problem. If so, ensure that repairs are carried out as soon as possible, which in turn should alleviate the problem of you spending money on repairs. I will deal with management companies and the associated experiences a little later.

If you have an older property not covered by warranties you would still need to contact your management company or the person who is taking care of the property for you, but the difference is that cost will now come into play. Generally, no matter who you call, someone else will have to be contacted and depending upon the severity of the problem, possibly be called out to make good the repairs or damage. That is going to take time and your money. You would, in effect, be in the hands of the gods as to which contractor would be called out to assess, price and repair the problem.

If or when a problem did arise, another important area for consideration would be to ascertain if the problem appeared so serious or urgent that it had to be dealt with immediately, or could it be left for a while as you may wish to make alternative arrangements for repairs to be made. There are two aspects in relation to this, the first being that you may save a small fortune by making your own arrangements, and secondly you may wish to balance savings in expenditure against your reputation and that of your business.

As you become more established in this field, you will find that recommendation by word of mouth is an extremely important and very powerful tool to boost and generate income. It would be a great shame if your business reputation became tarnished due to failures in looking after the needs of your customers, or not paying attention to small, yet important, details.

Sooner or later, like any other property, something will malfunction, require attention or need repairing. In addition to that, depending upon age and use, the property will need decorating to maintain a high standard of cleanliness and appearance. Once again, this area, where significant savings can be made, will be addressed later.

I had now made an informed decision. Rather than purchase an older resale property, where things such as carpets and other major household items, may need replacing due to age and use and the décor may require immediate attention to make it look contemporary, warm and attractive, I would now concentrate my efforts on looking toward buying a new property. As outlined, the alternative would have been to buy a resale property and have to spend more time and money to bring it up to an acceptable standard.

Another very important factor in relation to why my decision fell on the side of buying a new property, was the fact that it would take time to build. During that time, I knew that I could actually make money on the property in two different ways. This will become very clear as you read on !

After making that decision I started to think about the actual property itself. What type of property should I look at? How big should it be? What were the essentials? What would make my property more desirable than others? What would guests require? How would I furnish the property? Again, the number of questions just grew and grew.

My research had highlighted that there were several types of properties available for short term rental.

The smallest and least expensive that I considered were basic Condominiums (Condo's) or, for all intents and purposes, small apartments.

The vast majority of condo's that I found in the realtor magazines and newspapers were generally resale and were incorporated in blocks of four or six. There was a stairwell leading off from the ground floor Condo's onto a first floor landing type area where each of the other properties in the block also had its own trash or bin cupboard. Upon entering a condo, the first impression would be that the property was very limited in size and space. A typical condo was made up of a small lounge with open plan kitchen leading onto a utility room, bathroom with a toilet, bath and shower unit and some had another separate toilet. This was described as one and a half bathrooms in the estate agent brochures. The condo's had either two or three bedrooms, one of which at least had a double or, as the Americans describe it, a full size bed. The remaining bedrooms contained twin beds, but there was obviously an option to change the contents of the bedrooms around, depending on what your requirements were. An additional bed could be found in the lounge where the sofa could be converted into a double bed.

I had immediate reservations about allowing guests to utilise a sofa bed for a number of reasons. The first was that, if I was staying at the property as a guest for two or three weeks and had to sleep on such a bed, I would not be happy. I would find it uncomfortable to say the least and privacy would be limited. There may be times when you would prefer to retire to bed for the evening when others wanted to remain up and about, which would again cause a problem.

The last reason that I came up with and one which was very important to me, was the aspect of hygiene. I would prefer not to have to use the sofa bed for guests as you never know what might happen to it, particularly when it is located in the living room.

To have it damaged, and putting it bluntly, the very unpleasant thought of it being soiled by whatever means by someone was something which I would not tolerate either for me as the owner or for any other guests that would be living in the property.

Some of the condos advertised for sale on the resale market did appear quite well presented and on the face of it quite well maintained, however, only closer inspection would really identify any problems. All of the condo's which were on the market were furnished to varying standards and this, together with the location, was reflected in the price of the property.

Furnishing a rental home can be achieved in a number of ways, which again, I will explain a little later.

In my opinion, one of the main drawbacks of a condo was the fact that because of the type of property that it was, it did not have its own private heated swimming pool with a pool screen, which to me, was an essential element of a rental home. The ground floor condo's only had a very small patio area and the others in the building only had a small balcony, which was extremely limited in space.

The complex where these types of property can be found normally only had an open air, communal swimming pool, which at the time rarely had pool heating. These types of pool did not normally come with a pool screen either.

A pool screen is basically a metal frame which is covered in a very fine mesh which prevents any bugs from getting into the enclosed area whilst you are swimming or lying by the pool. This is not normally a problem during the day, but come evening time when a lot of the bugs such as mosquitoes, come out to play, a pool screen is essential to prevent you being on the bugs evening meal menu. This means that you can stay up all night, if you so desire, and have drinks around the pool with friends, and you would be relatively free from bugs and pests. At first the sight of a pool screen can seam slightly unusual and a little off putting, but its benefits would soon be found. For the sun lovers out there, don't be put off as you can still get a sun tan when inside the pool screen.

It became obvious to me that the only benefit in buying a condo was the fact that the price of the property and the initial outlay would be significantly less than buying a house of some description.

This of course was an individual thought and opinion as everyone is different and we all have different desires and financial parameters to work to. It was also very obvious to me that condo's had severe limitations in relation to the number of people that it could comfortably sleep. It would also impact upon the guests as they would be living on top of each other for the duration of their stay, as space was again at a premium and privacy, as mentioned, was limited.

As rental properties are regulated and required to be licensed, the maximum number of people who could reside in the property at any one time would be between six and eight, depending on the size of the property itself, and, of course, whatever the local licensing authorities view would be.

That fact would have a direct bearing on marketing the property and severe implications on the amount of income that it would generate.

My conclusion in relation to a condo was, yes, it would save me money in the short term in relation to initial outlay, however, this would again be false economy, as this type of property was arguably less attractive than a detached property and I would be restricting myself in relation to the amount of potential income that I would generate from it. In addition, the year on year increase in value of the property would probably be a lot less, in real terms, in comparison with that of a detached property.

So, by process of elimination, that was another decision made. Some would say that anyone who owns even a condo in Florida should consider themselves very fortunate and that is very true indeed, however, I had to look at and remain focused on the bigger picture. A condo would certainly never fulfil my dream of financial success, which would prove to be so significant, that it would change my lifestyle for good. It would not be a condo for me.

I had now made informed decisions that I would not buy a resale property nor would I buy a condo, and it was irrelevant whether they would be new or resale because of the restrictions and limitations that they would impose upon me.

The business plan and the blueprint for the type of property that I should purchase was now firmly in my mind. I found that my conclusion was hard to believe. In what was a relatively short space of time in my life, I had taken stock of what the future had in store for me and decided to take drastic action to make sure that I was in control and able to steer a course to ensure a very pleasant future indeed. There was no doubt in my mind. I was now sure that I should be looking toward a new build detached property, and it was essential that it had its very own heated swimming pool, and the pool deck area would be covered by a pool screen. Who would have thought that I would be doing such a thing in a foreign land almost four and a half thousand miles away?

Some may find it a frightening and very daunting prospect or experience, however, I have to say that I found the whole concept very exciting and completely different to the kind of excitement that I was used too.

My reasons for preferring a larger, detached property were that, in the short term, it would be a very attractive sales feature when marketing the property for rental. In particular, it would allow for example, either large families or two sets of friends to take a holiday together. Due to the sheer size of the property, more than one family could stay very comfortably in the villa at any one time. This, of course, would make the cost of the overall holiday much cheaper and therefore, more accessible for more potential guests. Also, on a lesser degree, if people were inclined to become more boisterous whilst staying in the property it would be less noisy for any neighbours. One of the most important factors as to why I had arrived at this conclusion was that, in the long term, the value of the property, which would also take into account those three very important words of location, location, location, would hopefully increase at a greater rate than a property such as a condo.

As I continued with my research, I started to receive mail from property companies with whom I had spoken. They all wanted my business. The invitations from such companies came in thick and fast, all of them wanted me to go to Florida to see for myself what was on offer. A lot of the property companies used the incentive of providing potential buyers with a villa, which was free of charge for one week, if they travelled to Florida and bought property with that particular company, basically, what became known as an 'inspection visit'. The only catch was that if you did not buy property, you were required to pay the property company for the one week rental, for the time you stayed in the villa. A number of other companies whom, for example, were selling holiday accommodation in Spain and Portugal, also contacted me with very similar offers.

I looked into this specific area with some detail and spoke with a number of people who were either thinking of buying property, or, who in fact had bought property. I was amazed at how different people had so many different views on the same subject. Based upon what I had been told by some, I was also totally amazed at how so many people put so much trust and faith in someone or some company with whom they had never met or had dealings with in the past. Some people were actually willing, and indeed bought property, with companies or through representatives whom they knew nothing or very little about. I found it hard to believe that some people were quite willing to sign on the dotted line for a property apparently without fully understanding the implications or the small print contained in the array of documentation.

I think the most amazing thing to me was the sheer number of people who, without any experience, guidance, advice or knowledge of the American property development market, and sometimes after only a single meeting with these company representatives in England, could look at a site or development plan, glossy brochures, a price list, then actually sign up to buy a house. Some of these buyers had, like myself, never even been to America before and there they were signing their lives away into this massive and unknown financial abyss. Some had never even spoken with anyone else about it. Personally, I just found this absolutely incredible.

We are talking about seriously high amounts of money being spent. Some people had re-mortgaged their homes in England or were using their pension funds to finance the purchase and it was obvious whilst talking with some individuals that they did not fully appreciate how they were going to undertake running or operating such a property and venture. They had absolutely no business plan or infrastructure in place to get them on their way, and my view was that, as they were not prepared, they were certainly going to run, full steam ahead, into difficulties. All that some could see was this dream of having a property abroad, but it appeared clear to me that they had not thought this through. This is where the romantic spin of what some people may see on television or in the glossy magazines takes over their mindset completely. It's that warm and fuzzy feeling in full flow !

This, to me, was extremely high risk to say the least and I did not know how these people could sleep in their beds at night with such a huge financial burden hanging over them and without any kind of business plan formulated. Maybe they did sleep because at that time, all that they could see was the fact that they would have a dream holiday home somewhere abroad, which they could visit in months to come. It was also distinctly possible that the reality of trying to actually successfully manage the property had not sunk in at that time, and one thing was for certain, and that was they had not yet encountered any problems with it.

A common theme that I found with some people who were buying property was the misconception that the management company would run the property for them, all their bills would be paid and everything would be just fine. This, to me, just did not ring true. Why was I so suspicious? Why was this so easy? Was this why so many people had failed in the past, lost their properties and considerable sums of money to go with it? Once again my mind was racing ahead.

Maybe I was too cautious with my money and maybe I was too untrusting of people whom I knew little or nothing about. This, in my mind, was not a bad stance to take. There was, however, one thing that I did know and that was I had undertaken considerable research into this idea and I was going into this with my eyes wide open. I did not wish to fall victim to some unscrupulous property dealer and lose my hard earned cash.

My overriding thought amongst all others, at this stage was, would I buy a house or business for that matter, in my home country without first seeing what I was buying, where it was located, what it looked like or how it operated. The answer was a definite and resolute no, I certainly would not.

So the offers and invitations continued to pour in from the various property companies. I soon had a very large pile of shiny magazines lying on the floor of the smallest bedroom of my home which I had now designated as my office.

Another decision was now looming. What model or type of house should I choose?

Initially, I had thought about buying a new three bedroom detached house as at first I believed that it would be just big enough and well within my budget to make me feel comfortable and still have funds in reserve as my safety net. Baring in mind that I was still at home and had not yet been to America, I was working from colour brochures and plans of houses on new developments that I had not yet seen for myself. In reality, I had to ascertain what was on offer and what would the differences actually be in real terms. As I alluded too earlier, the more that I thought about it, the more it became clear to me that to buy a three bedroom property would be a mistake. This was based on the fact that a three bedroom property would once again require to be licensed for this particular type of business and it would have a maximum occupancy of no more than eight people. If eight people were to stay in the property, where would they sleep? It would mean that six could be divided into the three bedrooms and the other two would have to sleep on the sofa bed in the living room. As I have already mentioned, I did not want the sofa bed used in that way for all the reasons that I have already outlined.

In addition to the sleeping arrangements, if eight people had to live together in a three bedroom house for two or three weeks they would be living in each others pockets, as once again, space and privacy would be at a premium. One more thought was, how many bathrooms would a three bedroom property have? Floor plans of that type of property suggested that it may only have an en-suite bathroom in a master bedroom and only one other separate bathroom for the remainder of the household to use. If eight people were staying there at any one time, how much of a problem would that present to them and how much of a drawback would it be for me when marketing the property especially when trying to entice guests to re-book with me?

I was now starting to move away from the idea of a three bedroom property and looking toward buying a four bedroom instead. That raised the next area of dilemma. My research indicated that, in the main, the detached properties available for short term rental came in two different categories. The first being the bungalow type of property and the second being the more conventional type of house with the bedrooms located on more than one floor. I was immediately drawn toward the more conventional house with the upstairs bedrooms, as at home that was what I was used too and those properties looked everything that I had dreamed about. They looked magnificent in the brochures and videos that I had been shown by the property company representatives. They had really tried to push that type of property as being the best for short term rental and when I had asked why, I was told that it was ideal as the bedrooms were upstairs and out of the way and generally there was more free space in the house.

Let's just have a close look at those comments. The company representatives were really pushing these houses for sale.........
I wonder why?

You may call me a cynic, however was it true what their sales pitch was outlining and suggesting or was it, as I have already pointed out, the bigger the house they sold the bigger the commission they could receive?

I came to the conclusion that it would be very nice indeed to own a huge house in Florida but a number of reasons kept my feet firmly on the ground. First of all those lovely big homes were very, very expensive and out of my financial league. Secondly, baring in mind that my business would be initially marketed toward British families who wanted to take a holiday in Florida, but keep their costs to a minimum, would the high rental cost of that type of property, which I would have to charge to cover my overheads, be prohibitive and put it beyond the financial reach of some families who had a limited budget to work within. Thirdly, the overheads on such a property would vastly reduce my profit margin. Finally, there was something else that I had noticed on the presentation videos that I had been shown. A vast majority of the houses with bedrooms upstairs had open stairs with a small wall or hand rail which opened onto landing areas which looked down onto the living area. Once again, only a small wall or rail was actually preventing anyone from falling over the top down into the living area. The height of which obviously varied, and by my basic calculations, I estimated it to be generally about fifteen feet high from the balcony area of the first floor to the ground. It was clear to see that an accident was quite possible, especially if a child was in high spirits and over excited on holiday. It did not bear thinking about the possible consequences of someone being injured in my home and additionally any possible litigation that may arise from such an incident.

Some people may consider that those thoughts were a little extreme, however, others may also realise the problems that it could cause both to the injured person and the property owner. Litigation is an expensive and uncomfortable word, no matter in which country it occurs in. Those types of concerns may not be a problem for some property owners, but I was looking closely at the whole picture, and I mean from every aspect that I could think of.

As a side issue one other thing was worthy of note. It would certainly cost more, in terms of time and money, to clean a property of that size whenever clients left the house and energy bills, for example, to keep such a property cool using the essential air conditioning would increase. When it came to maintenance, those inevitable repairs, replacing of furnishings and decorating would cost a lot more too. These were more things to take money out of my pocket, which was definitely not what I wanted.

Through this process of elimination I was by now looking toward buying a new four bedroom bungalow type property, which included its own private heated swimming pool.

Many things had swayed me toward this decision including price, value for money, sufficient bedroom and communal space to allow two families to holiday together, thereby keeping their costs down, and adequate bathroom availability. In addition and very importantly, with the property all on ground level, there would be easy access for everyone, especially for anyone who may have a disability. Overall it would also be easier to maintain such a property. This type of property also negated the problem of children and dangerous balcony's !

The private heated swimming pool was a very important marketing feature indeed, and one which just about everyone asks about when going on holiday to Florida.

I now had a very good idea of what I was looking for and I still had not set foot in America. It was time to find a suitable company or realtor (estate agent) to deal with.

I was very interested in taking the opportunity of travelling to Florida and staying, free of charge, in a villa for a week whilst I looked for a suitable property to purchase. After speaking with various realtors and getting the feel for what they were saying and how it was being said, I came to another conclusion and that was I did not want, nor would I allow, any pressure sales pitch from anyone. I have seen and heard of such pressures placed on people through aggressive marketing by sales staff, similar to that of some unscrupulous time share companies who have been highlighted in the media in recent years, and that was something that I would not allow myself to be subjected too.

All I needed now was to find a suitable, reliable and trustworthy licensed realtor who would be able and willing to provide that personal touch and who would not attempt to place any pressure or influence on me whatsoever. If I was pressured in any way I would immediately discard the services of that particular person or company. It was therefore essential that, before I travelled out to Florida, that I should identify a suitable person with whom to conduct business.

The words 'easier said than done' sprung to mind.

You may say where and how do I do that? I started by speaking to various realtors and asking a lot of questions, firstly about the mysterious world of property purchase in Florida, and secondly, more probing questions about what would be in it for them. I wanted to ask that particular question just to see how they reacted and how forthcoming they were. Some were a little more 'cagey' than others and they were discarded immediately. The reason being that, if they could not be up front, honest and open with me at this early stage of enquiring about buying a property with them, then I seriously doubted that they would be the best person to act in my interests in the long term.

I asked a number of realtors to supply me with details of clients whom they had assisted to buy property in the recent past or if they could get those people to contact me. Once again some were forthcoming and others were not. Those who would not were once again discarded as my suspicions were raised as to what they may be trying to hide. I then made enquiries with recent clients of the realtors that were left on my short list.

Although I accept that everyone is different and all of us have our own standards, views and opinions, I still believe that personal recommendation goes along way to re-assuring you, the potential buyer, that there is a stronger likelihood of receiving a good service. A happy and satisfied customer is more likely to be open and positive about the service received and the decisions that they made and can assist others in making their informed decisions. The only caveat being, try and make sure that the person who is recommending the service is not somehow professionally involved with the person whom they are recommending. That may sound a little difficult to do, but if you dig deep enough you may be able to confirm or eliminate your suspicions. Try and speak with other property owners, realtors, site development agents or any management company that are also recommended as they may be able to throw some light onto the subject. If there are internet web sites for the realtors you are looking at, have a good browse through as they may have connections with other companies or corporations with whom you could enquire. These are just a few ideas that you could use to identify a suitable and reliable realtor who will be able to provide the right service for you.

Its not that I am a totally untrusting person, its just that I would not like to be 'ripped off' by someone, and especially by a person who is thousands of miles away whose only interest is lining their own pockets with other peoples money, especially, my hard earned money.

I had now identified a realtor that I was happy to deal with and had several conversations with that person on the telephone as she lived in Florida. I was offered and accepted a free week in a villa in Florida in order that I could get the feel for the whole thing and be able to conduct business and view property that was available and on offer.

At this point I should say that my partner at the time, and now my wife, was very understanding about the whole thing. I was going to travel out to Florida at relatively short notice and spend a week in 'The Sunshine State' and, unfortunately, she could not travel with me due to other commitments. Never mind, I would really miss her but as they say......onwards and upwards !

On this occasion it was going to be purely a business trip to get things up and running. I would also be reminded on a fairly regular basis by my wife as to how understanding she had been !

So, the BMW was now for sale and I had a number of people interested in buying the car. I had sufficient funds available to put down as an initial deposit, on a refundable basis, to temporarily reserve a lot on a new house, which would give a few weeks breathing space to realise the sale of the car into hard cash and I had everything ready to go. I had all my documentation to show that I was a good risk to any lending company and I had my glossy brochures, floor plans, price lists and maps. I also packed a very important piece of equipment which I would use on a very regular basis – my pocket calculator.

Now the adventure was really about to start. It was time to book a flight to Florida.

CHAPTER 5

Breakfast in America

As I looked out of the cabin window during the aircrafts descent into Orlando Sanford Airport, I could see that it was a beautiful day in sunny Florida. Clear blue sky and sunshine were the order of that day and, as my research had revealed, on most other days in the year. We were now over land and as I looked down to visually explore this strange but magical part of the world I recall my immediate thoughts as being what a fantastic, yet unusual looking land I was flying in to.

Florida was obviously a vast area and the amazing thing that sticks out in my mind was that there appeared to be beautiful residential housing estates that were surrounded by what I could only describe as swampland and lakes. My research into Florida had clearly identified how the land was made up, but to actually see it was something else. The contrast was bizarre, lovely detached houses surrounded with what appeared from the air to be a jungle. Strange looking swamp trees growing out of water-ways and lakes with beautiful white large billed birds of some description flying over them. I snapped back into reality as we flew past what appeared to be a huge modern power station with two or three very large chimneys which were so big that they had numerous strobe warning lights attached to the side of them. This was from one extreme to the other. Swampland which had probably not changed in thousands, if not millions, of years to the technology of the present and the future. As we flew over what looked like very flat land I could see the strange mix of areas. From swamp land to shopping malls from orange groves to golf courses, it had it all. This really did feel like an adventure now. I remember the feeling of excitement coming over me as we made our way down from the skies on our final approach to the airport. I was desperate to get off the aircraft and explore this magical, yet mysterious part of the world that I had never ever set foot in before.

The flight from Manchester had been uneventful and very pleasant indeed. It had taken just under nine hours. I had arrived at Orlando Sanford Airport in Florida and as the aircraft taxied to the terminal building I adjusted my wrist-watch to read five hours behind UK time.

As I looked out of the cabin window, I could not get enough of what was going on in my new surroundings.

During the flight I had many thoughts about what I was about to do. I had that feeling of excitement and anticipation, combined with an element of caution to ensure that I made all the right decisions. I had researched this idea long and hard, I had asked all the questions that I could think of, and more. I had got all the answers that I needed and there was one thing which I knew. I had never been so positive about something in all my life. I knew that I was doing the right thing and that this venture was about to change my whole life style. As I sit here and relay my experiences to you here and now, I can still sense that feeling of excitement running through my body just as it did as I sat on the aircraft. To be in a position where you know that the rest of your life is going to dramatically change for the better, is an extraordinary feeling. I knew that it was very early days to have such a feeling, but I was so enthusiastic about my plans and absolutely determined to succeed that I knew with that kind of physical and mental drive, combined with the passion for the nicer things in life that money can and does buy, that I was going to be successful. My future was in my hands. That was and still is a great feeling to experience.

As I walked from the aircraft I recall my first taste of the Floridian heat. It was an absolute scorcher of a day. Clear blue sky and the sun was blazing down. It was July and it was over

100 degrees. I really needed to get out of the trousers that I had been travelling in and get into my shorts, just like the local people. Even though I was there on business, there was no reason at all why I should not take every opportunity to top up the suntan.

It was like being in an open air sauna but I was definitely not complaining. That's what Florida is all about. Great weather, great sights, great places to go and always plenty to do. I knew that I had plenty to do on this particular visit to the Sunshine State. As I walked through the terminal building I remember thinking to myself well here you are in America - the land of opportunity - and this was my opportunity. All I wanted to do was collect my rental car and drive, just to see and feel everything around me.

I had to admire how friendly the airport staff were. That was the first time I heard those typical Floridian words, which will stay with me forever. They came from an airport porter who provided me with a trolley for my luggage at the carousel. As I said thank you to him he replied "You're welcome sir, have a nice day ".

Have a nice day ! That was a phrase that I would here all the time in Florida but did they really mean it? Whether they meant it or not, just about everyone that you speak to in Florida will say it to you and they appear to mean what they say. What a refreshing change !

Orlando Sanford Airport (SFB) is one of the two main airports in central Florida. The other being Orlando International Airport (MCO).

Orlando International is the main airport and is located east of Kissimmee. It terms of time, it is approximately thirty minutes from the areas of Orlando and Kissimmee. It is a very modern and major international airport and covers a vast area. It has monorail transportation system from the terminals and all of the usual types of shops to pass the time away whilst waiting for your flight.

Orlando Sanford Airport is located north of Orlando and is approximately forty five minutes away from the main tourism area of Kissimmee. Once again it is a very modern airport but is much smaller and has fewer facilities than Orlando International.

This airport was built as an overflow airport to accommodate the increasing number of foreign tourists to the area, and takes in the vast amount of charter flights from the United Kingdom.

My many visits to Florida would soon show me that both Orlando Sanford and Orlando International airports were extremely passenger friendly with good signage and very helpful staff. Once you leave the aircraft, collect your luggage and pass through immigration and customs its time to pick up your rental vehicle.

At Orlando Sanford it could not be any easier. As you walk out of the front doors of the terminal building the main vehicle rental companies are right there, only a few meters away.

At Orlando International as you make your way to the front of the terminal building you will see a long line of assorted vehicle rental company check-in desks.

The format at both airports is the same. All you do is present your car hire voucher, if you have one, to the staff at the check-in desk who will check your details against your passport and driving licence and then complete some basic paperwork. This procedure normally only takes five minutes or so to complete. I had pre-booked my car hire in the UK, received my car hire voucher and paid all of the insurances and taxes before I arrived in Florida so there would be no nasty and unexpected little financial surprises in relation to any extra charges. Before I had booked the rental car, I had heard all about upgrading your vehicle once you arrived in Florida and horror stories about some people who had to pay for additional insurances and taxes upon arrival and collection of their rental vehicle. This practise, in the main, affected tourists, who thought that they had a great deal on some fly-drive holiday packages, but either did not know or maybe had not been made fully aware, of the additional local charges and minimum levels of insurance that were required in Florida. If they did not pay those additional miscellaneous fees they would not be able to collect their rental vehicle.

I had carried out extensive research into the upgrading of rental vehicles and found that, as I wanted to drive a fairly comfortable sized car, financially it would be best for me to book and pay for a basic economy car and once I arrived to collect it at the check-in desk I would try to 'haggle' or negotiate an upgrade for far less than the advertised cost. I did not know if it would work but unless you try something you will never know.

This was business and it was no time to be shy. Polite, professional, tactful and diplomatic yes, but shy, definitely not.

The attendant at the check-in desk seemed a reasonable sort of a guy so I asked him if there were any deals available for upgrades. He gave me the costings for the various vehicles but that still seemed to me to be a little too steep a price to pay.

Time for the haggle and, without going into all of the detail, it worked and fairly successfully even if I may say so myself. The bottom line was that for the cost of an upgrade to the next vehicle on the rental specification list above an economy car I managed to jump seven grades to a full size family car. I was very pleased with that deal and used the same method whenever I travelled to Florida with varying degrees of success. I did not always jump seven grades, but I always made considerable improvement on my rental vehicles, for well under the advertised price. It worked for me and I have no doubt that it worked for others.

As a side issue, as I became more successful in my venture, each and every time that I travelled to Florida on business, as way of a small reward to myself for the work that I put in, I always rented a Sports Utility Vehicle (SUV 4x4). I have certainly not been extravagant with my hard earned cash and everything that I have earned has been reinvested one way or another into the business, however, there is one thing that I have done over the years. That one thing is to set my own targets and once I have achieved those goals, I reward myself in some small way. This was just one of those small ways of self reward, and the price of renting such a vehicle was always subject to 'haggle' and negotiation to get the cheapest price possible.

So, this very pleasant gentleman at the vehicle check-in desk who had just 'offered' me a great little deal provided me with all of the documentation in relation to the vehicle rental that I needed for my stay in Florida. The documents were essentially, the rental agreement, which I would need should I be stopped by the police or be involved in an accident, heaven forbid, and that other very important piece of paper - a map. I was then given a car park lot number, directed to the car lot where you find that particular numbered bay and there you have it, your rental vehicle awaits. Nice and easy - nothing could be easier and extremely customer friendly.

There is a point as to why I have explained my first experience of vehicle rental in Florida, and once again, relate this to your circumstances and the location of your desired property.

I was particularly interested in the procedures in relation to vehicle hire as this was going to be another way where I would generate income for my business. At this point I was just taking everything in. I was the equivalent of a human sponge just soaking up all of this information and I saw this type of information as an investment for the future.

Never miss an opportunity is what I firmly believe in, and this certainly would be another opportunity for me to generate even more income.

There it was parked in the bay waiting for me. As it said on my amended car hire voucher an 'FDAR'.

An 'FDAR' was a full size car, with either two or four doors. This car was a deep red coloured four door 'Dodge Intrepid'. It was a family type car but looked very sporty and very comfortable. That would be perfect to travel around Central Florida for the week.

After thoroughly checking the car over for any damage before I drove it away I threw my suitcase into the 'trunk' and got into the drivers seat. Very impressive I thought and very spacious. It had all the luxuries of a top of the range car, but this really was only your standard type of rental car. Nevertheless, it had automatic transmission which would make life very easy, a good radio / CD player and probably the most important thing of all – air conditioning. I was ready to go.

Before I travelled out to Florida I obviously knew that I would have to drive to get about so I had researched the Florida highway code very well. It's one thing reading about driving in a foreign country and completely another actually doing it for real. The order of the day for me was too take it easy. This type of general information would be another way of assisting my customers and I certainly would literally go that extra mile to help them. In general, attention to detail was important to me and the overall way that I researched and prepared every aspect of the business and the package of services that I would supply, would help put me ahead of any competition that I may have.

I donned my sunglasses started up the car and I was off, following the prepared directions to where I would pick up the keys for my rented villa.

My first impressions were that I was driving a good car on good open roads with plenty of room to manoeuvre. Cross roads, traffic lights and junctions were a little strange but I survived. I hadn't had a 'wreck' in the first few miles so I knew that was a good sign at least. No problem.

My destination was a property management company office just off the busy Irlo Bronson Highway 192, near the beautiful and very exclusive town of Celebration.

Celebration, which is a residential town and not a theme park as many people believe, is a place that became very significant to both my wife and I. It became a very special place, and for me it was a place of great importance, but that is something which I will go into greater detail about later.

My journey took me south along a road named the Central Florida Greeneway 417. This was a typical American dual carriageway with absolutely loads of space, few cars and a speed limit of 55 MPH. Another tip I had received before going to Florida was watch out for State Troopers as speeding fines can be very expensive. My eyes were peeled as they say, and yes, the State Troopers were definitely out there, just watching and waiting. I'm sure that they would be nice guys though there was nothing personal in the fact that I did not wish to be on the business end of any encounter with one of them.

I soon found out why roads such as the 417 were relatively quiet and traffic free and that was because it was a toll road and most locals apparently prefer to use any other road than have to pay.

So there I was just a few minutes out of Orlando Sanford Airport heading south on the 417 in my 'Dodge Intrepid' on a red hot, beautiful sunny day with the air-con working overtime to keep me cool. The only thing that was missing was some good music. It was time to tune in to Floridian radio.

This was my first experience of driving in Florida and I was feeling good as I approached my first toll booth. The sign flashed and directed me to either take a lane for pre-paid passes or to the toll booths were I would pay cash. This booth required me to pay $1-25. That wasn't bad for traffic free motoring. I pulled up at the booth where I was met with a big smile from a really nice black lady. I handed her the dollar twenty five, she thanked me and beamed out to me "You have a wonderful day sir"

I thanked her very much and bid her a good day too. I felt like one of the locals already !

As I drove away from the booth I forgot one thing that I had been told by an accountant in England, and that was to get receipts for anything and everything that I spent money on in relation to my business venture for accurate records and tax purposes. A dollar twenty five would certainly not break the bank or make much difference for my tax returns, but I would certainly bare that advice in mind for the future. I may as well get into the habit of collecting receipts from the start. It would keep everything just right and would be financially beneficial for me later on, at the end of the tax year.

In between the vast expanses of undeveloped marsh, swampland and farmers fields I could see what looked like very attractive residential housing estates just off the 417. It was an amazing contrast that I could quite clearly see now. As you fly into Orlando you can obviously see the terrain below, but to actually see it at ground level is something else. It was basically swampland with weird and wonderful trees, bushes and vine type plants growing out at strange angles. There were beautiful white wading birds all over the place and I wondered what other creatures were living in that swampland neighbourhood. There were bound to be alligators and snakes after all they had inhabited the area for thousands, if not millions, of years and no doubt they would still be there in abundance...somewhere !

The wildlife in Florida can be fascinating, however, I knew from the start that I would have to be very careful in what I said to guests to ensure that I did not frighten them out of their wits ! I did not want to alarm them in any way, I just needed to make them aware of their surroundings and what they could expect to see. As it happened, I would later learn that local wildlife was a topic of many clients conversation when they enquired about renting holiday property in Florida.

The climate in Florida is sub tropical and therefore it would naturally attract a wide and extremely varied range of creatures. In fact there are several places to visit where you can actually see such creatures. Gators' can be seen in the wild if you go to the right places and look carefully enough.

Another early tip then, don't frighten your customers, tell them the truth, but be realistic. Be positive and reassure them that it will be a great experience that they will never forget !

On a completely different note, I saw that every so often along the highway there were huge billboards or advertising hoardings situated at the side of the road, and I mean huge. These were the biggest advertising signs that I had ever seen. They say everything in America is bigger and better, well these signs definitely fitted into the category of 'bigger'. I was soon to find out that food was arguably the most talked about and advertised subject in America. No matter where you were, you could not escape from it, whether it be on the TV, car radio, bill boards, newspapers and so on. I also found that a vast amount of good restaurants, diners and any other outlet where food could be bought also offered discount vouchers or coupons to their customers, which gave, for example 10%, 15% or even more off the total bill. When you entered any such place, the first thing that the server would ask for was your discount voucher or coupon. If you did not have one, they looked at you as though you were stupid and quietly suggested that you go back outside to where there are many open and free advertising stands and select a book of coupons which included a voucher for that particular restaurant or outlet.

This was something that, in the UK, we were generally not used to. It soon became apparent to me that any family who were on holiday could save a considerable amount of money by using these free vouchers or coupons every time they had a meal. Over a two week period, for example, this would allow them to either buy or do something extra special or reduce the overall cost of their holiday. For anyone who may think that this may be a 'class thing' or that they may feel a little uncomfortable or that there is some sort of stigma attached by even thinking about producing a coupon for a discounted meal, forget it. It is natural and quite normal in Florida and what is more, it is expected. There is absolutely no stigma attached to it whatsoever.

This was undoubtedly a positive area to explore, and for me personally, I would create a win-win situation from it. Invariably, people always remember discounts, reductions in price and bargains. This to me was something else that would assist me in selling my services to my customers. You will see later the many ways in which you can stand out from your competitors and there are many ways in which you can do so !

After collecting the keys to the villa, I followed the directions and found the property that I would be staying at for the week. The following quote is one which I have referred to over and over again for many years and has always been at the forefront of my mind. Since launching into this venture, it has been especially relevant and of great importance to my business profile, and that is, You never get a second chance to make a first impression !

My first impression of this particular villa was that it was a relatively old, tired looking, four bedroom detached villa, which had clearly seen better days. It did however have a private swimming pool, which was a good size and views to the rear of the house. It was located in an area and neighbourhood which I would best describe as a place where I would not be buying my property.

The villa was situated in an area which was zoned for both short term rental and residential property, and the general impression was that the area was unkempt. In my view, it would not be particularly attractive for guests who had paid a considerable sum of money for a special holiday. If a guest came to this area, the chances are that they would not want to return to it ever again. That would certainly affect my business and my reputation, as everything that I did would be built upon high standards and a first class, quality, prompt and professional service.

I wanted that 'wow' factor for my guests when they first arrived and saw the high quality and standard of my rental holiday home, and not a feeling of disappointment that they would probably have had if they had paid for accommodation such as this.

The other very important factor that I picked up on straight away with this particular villa was that, in my opinion, the area was too far away from the main tourist attractions where most people wanted to be.

Although, initially, these comments and views may appear very negative, it was in reality a very positive experience, as I immediately knew what I wanted and I certainly knew that I did not want anything like this.

I had arrived at the villa around 7.30pm and, although it was still very hot outside, upon entering I found that the air conditioning had kept the rooms inside down to a very pleasant and somewhat cooling temperature indeed. I looked around and saw that two or three of the light bulbs had blown and that my first impression of the inside of the property was that it could do with a good cleaning and a lick of paint ! I checked out the refrigerator and saw that the only thing inside it was plenty of ice. I knew that the ice would come in handy for my drinks around the pool on an evening.

Just before I arrived at the villa, I had seen a supermarket named Publix, which was only a short distance from where I was staying. My first mission was to find it again and stock up on some essential supplies. Publix was a large supermarket chain that I would visit on many occasions, along with two other very well known names, Wal-Mart and Home Depot.

Home Depot was very similar in appearance to B&Q back in the UK.

Publix supermarkets seemed to be everywhere and had everything that you would ever need in way of provisions. I recall my first visit very clearly indeed, as I bought half a dozen light bulbs and a twelve pack of local beer. A bit of a mixed bag you might say, but there you go. I did also buy a few other essentials as well. The very fact that I had to buy light bulbs did concern me, as the property should have been checked before any guests had arrived. I know it is only a small thing, but again, it is first impressions that count and this was lack of attention to detail by whoever was looking after that villa.

Wal-Mart was an amazing place to go shopping. It had some great bargains and, as a property owner, it would be one of the main places that I would go to on a regular basis. The reason being, that I could buy some very good quality products, without spending a small fortune on them and thereby keeping more money in my pocket.

Another early secret that I will share with you is, always remember, it is so important to achieve that wow factor from your guests when they arrive at your holiday home, but don't spend an absolute fortune on the contents. Remember, it is a holiday home so get the balance right.

The other thing about Wal-Mart was that it was the only supermarket that I had been in where I could buy a loaf of bread, pint of milk, a speedboat and a shotgun under one roof. I suppose that's America for you !

I decided to give the speedboat and shotgun a miss !

I had decided not to go too far on the first night. I wanted to make sure that I was ready to meet the realtor the following morning, as arranged prior to leaving the UK. I wanted a clear head and have as much information at hand as possible.

By the time I got back, it was around 9.30pm, so what could be better than supper around the pool. I switched on the swimming pool underwater lights, had a very relaxing swim and then had my evening meal around quite a nice pool. Now I could see the benefit of the large pool screens. Sub tropical climate and not a bug in sight !

I could get used to this kind of lifestyle !

CHAPTER 6

Making and meeting the contacts

Nine o'clock sharp, the doorbell rang. As arranged, there she was, my realtor. I had awoken around 5am, which was nothing unusual for me, and got up around 6.00am. My mind was racing about the day ahead. It was a very real, and as expected, a totally different kind of excitement that I had been used too.

After speaking on the telephone many times, and seeing her face on her internet web site, it was good to actually meet her in person. No time was wasted and after exchanging the usual pleasantries, we left the villa and got into her SUV (Sports Utility Vehicle). Everybody in Florida seemed to be driving an SUV for some reason, probably because the cost of petrol at that time was so low.

We had covered much ground during our telephone conversations, and, as my time was limited to seven days, this greatly assisted both her and me, as it narrowed things down and focussed my attention on certain new developments.

We spent the day travelling between developments and I was taking in as much information as possible. This information included gathering as much of the free literature from the show houses, or models as they are known out there, as I could. My intention being that, at the end of each day, I could sit around the pool at my rental villa and decide on the best way forward.

During the morning of the first day, we had visited, amongst a number of others, a new development, which was just in the process of being launched by the developer. The site was just off Highway 27, in Polk County, and was approximately 15 minutes from Walt Disney World and some of the other major theme parks and attractions. This particular area around Highway 27 was where the four counties of Polk, Lake, Orange and Osceola met, and it had become known as The Four Corners. Virtually this entire area had been zoned for short term rental properties, and I believed that this certainly would be one of the more desirable areas to be located. I was thinking well ahead in terms of both attracting guests and repeat bookings, along with the potential for a healthy growth in the value of property.

When people were going to Florida on holiday, they all seemed to say that they were either going to, or wanted to be, in Kissimmee. This new development was very, very close to that area, and as such, the location seemed just about right. I had my maps at the ready and it was clear to see that this area was just ripe for further development. There was a huge amount of land just waiting to be bought up and I tried to visualise what the area would look like and how it could change over forthcoming years. To me, one thing was certain and this had been borne out during my research. That was, people on holiday including myself, want things to be nice and easy, enjoyable and stress free. Baring in mind that Florida was arguably the family holiday capital of the world, this to me screamed out that any property within say twenty minutes of Walt Disney World and other major theme parks, would always be in great demand.

Not to be too scientific about this, however, I worked out the scale of the map and did some basic calculations as to time, speed and distance and drew a circle on the map with the centre of it being Walt Disney World. Anything located within that circle was probably less than twenty minutes travelling time to the theme parks.

That part of Highway 27 was well within that circle and I actually drove the route to measure and confirm my calculations in relation to the time and distance that it would be from Walt Disney World. This new development was approximately fifteen minutes travelling time. This was perfect, sufficiently close enough for ease and accessibility, yet sufficiently far enough away for peace and quiet and total relaxation around your own private swimming pool.

The development was only five minutes from the busy area of Highway 192, which had a vast amount of shopping malls, specialist discount shops and an unbelievable amount of places to eat out at very reasonable prices. This would certainly be popular with families. This location certainly looked and felt right.

When I took a good look at the development plans, the new estate looked very attractive indeed.

The area to be developed had been marked out, the wall around the estate had been built and the service road had been laid. Two large houses had already been built, and formed the show house area, and construction had started on four or five other homes. Those properties were all different in size and shape and would obviously clearly illustrate what was on offer and the standard of work that could be expected from this developer. I found out that those houses would eventually be Turn Key properties, i.e. when those homes were released for sale by the builder, buyers would literally be able to purchase those properties and when they took possession of the keys and entered, it was a complete package, including all of the furniture that was inside. In effect, you would be able to buy what you could see.

I scrutinised the plans for this development, and as I was one of the very first to be interested in buying property on that estate, I could virtually choose whatever plot of land, or 'lot' as they called it, that I wanted.

To cut a very long story short, I visited many new developments and, just so that I was absolutely sure, I also saw a few four bedroom resale properties.

My initial thoughts about resale property were correct, and without going into detail, I eliminated those properties straight away. At my request, we returned to the development off Highway 27. My realtor and I spoke with the realtor in the show home who was actually employed by the developer.

This meeting was very useful indeed. I managed to get a good overall picture of how the development would look when completed, and of all the different stages in between, as various phases of the estate would be released.

I liked what I saw and the estate appeared to be well thought out. All of the properties for sale would be detached homes with their own private swimming pools. The homes had plenty of space between them, so privacy was maintained and most were not really overlooked by any other property at all. This was a major factor that I had considered in relation to guests not just having privacy in the home itself, but privacy whilst they enjoyed themselves around the private swimming pool as well.

There were a number of other factors why I favoured that particular development. They included, as previously mentioned, it was what became more commonly known as a gated community. It had a clubhouse and a communal swimming pool and it would also have a Home Owners Association.

The gated community would be a good selling feature to attract my guests. It meant that it was a safe place to be and appeared to be somewhat exclusive. It was not open to just anyone was the way it would be seen by guests and marketed by myself. The clubhouse, which included a small gymnasium, cable TV room and other features, was an ideal place for people to meet, and they could use the large communal swimming pool. This would also mean less wear and tear on my property, especially if there were more than one family on holiday together !

Initially, the Home Owners Association could be seen as a double edged sword. I spent some time thinking this over and, the way that I saw it was, the drawbacks could be seen as firstly, it was a mandatory membership, secondly, some association would be able to tell people what they could and could not do with their own property, and thirdly, it would cost villa owners money in way of membership contributions which would have to be paid out every month. The positive element to this association was that it actually had teeth to enforce local rules, regulations or bye-laws.

There would be benefits in this, which I believed, would far outweigh the negative points. As I alluded to earlier, it meant that if anyone on the estate did not take good care of their property or maintain it to the required or expected high standard, the association could take firm, positive and timely action against the home owner. This included ultimately, foreclosure on their home. Quite a powerful allie to have, albeit, that it would cost me money.

The association was a definite plus for me. The last thing that I wanted was for some owner to be allowed to let their property go to wreck and ruin, which could effect the whole image of the estate, and ultimately, my business. Remember what I said earlier about first impressions !

The other benefits included, as part of the monthly fees to the association, were that twice a month the lawns would be cut and maintained on each and every house on the estate, which ensured that things looked just right all the time and part of the monthly fee also went to maintain the communal swimming pool and clubhouse.

I had no problem with this, and all that I would have to do is factor that into my overall monthly expenditure, which would be reflected in my villa rental price structure.

I was happy with what I could visualise for the future, and now I had to concentrate on what type of property would most suit my requirements, and what would be within my overall budget?

The plans of the estate were very clear. All the lots were marked out on the plans and shown on a small scale model of the estate in one of the show homes. The plans outlined that all of the properties would be detached, the smallest property would be a 3 bedroom / 2 bathroom home and the largest would be a 5/6 bedroom property with something in the region of 4 or more bathrooms, depending upon individual requirements.

Obviously, the size of the lots differed accordingly, and the larger the lot, the larger the lot premium would be. In effect, you would have to pay the going rate for the best or larger plots. The lot premiums really did differ, and this was not only due to size but also whether it was south facing or overlooked what was described as a conservation area, a lake or other water feature for example.

I looked at the plans, and took into account the direction that the house would face, and very importantly, which way the pool deck would face to maximise sunshine around the pool. I also took into account the view from all angles, but again, in particular from the pool area as this would be where most of the time would be spent when guests were at the house. The final consideration was whether guests would be overlooked whilst sunbathing or whilst in the pool.

I saw a corner lot marked on the plan, and as I was one of the first to consider buying a home on this new development, I could have my pick. It looked just about perfect for my requirements, and amazingly it was quite a large lot but had a reasonable lot premium.

As this was America, I jumped into a golf cart or buggy as we know it which the realtor used to travel around the development and we went to have a look at the available lot. This particular mode of transport seemed to be common place on new developments, as I had seen quite a few on the estates that I had visited. I suppose that it was in keeping with the area, which is also known for its many fantastic golf courses. Although I personally do not play golf, this would be another great opportunity for me to increase my income. There are thousands of golf courses in Florida and there were many good class or championship golf courses located within just a few minutes from this estate.

Perfect in every respect, I thought. I had with me a bundle of architect's impressions of the different types of homes that would be built on this development and I took particular interest in a 4 bedroom bungalow type property. The dimensions were just right to fit onto this lot, and still leave plenty of land around it.

Very importantly, the price was certainly within my budget ! It became clear that both my realtor and the realtor representing the developer were quite friendly with one another and they had what appeared to be a very good working relationship. I was immediately cautious about this, however as it turned out, it actually assisted me in the long term and amongst other things I was able to provisionally reserve the lot that I had seen and in effect get first refusal on it.

I was fully aware that both of the realtors would make a commission out of me if I bought a house on that development and I accepted that, as after all, they were also in business to make money, just as I was. I was also aware that I could have dumped my original realtor and dealt direct with the developer's realtor, however at that time it would not have been to my advantage.

I then entered into full negotiation to get the best deal that I possibly could. My intention was to get as much as I could for my money and I was certainly looking for discounts whenever and wherever possible. One of the first impressions that you get in Florida, and this was apparent at the very start of my research, was the fact that you get an awful lot of property for your money, compared with here in the UK or in some European countries, for example. There I was, looking at a four bedroom / two bathroom detached property, with a huge kitchen, dining area, separate living area, private swimming pool and double garage for the fraction of the cost of a property in the UK, Spain or Portugal for example. Everything that I had seen in Florida was certainly impressive.

My first point of negotiation was the lot premium.

The premium was reasonable in any event, but I wanted to reduce it somehow. I was aware that I was in a strong position to barter as I knew that the realtor employed by the developer really needed to get house sales moving to get this development up and running. They also knew that I was a serious potential buyer with money in my pocket. I made it clear that if the deal was right, I was willing to put a deposit down. This, as money normally does, really got them going and like any other serious buyer I had their undivided attention.

As with the car hire experience when I had first arrived in Florida, we managed to carve out a deal on the lot premium, which saved me a few thousand dollars.

My initial thoughts in relation to how the actual mechanics of business worked were certainly confirmed. If you push hard enough, there will always be a deal available.

Through careful, polite but persistent negotiation, I had a tangible result. This, even though I say it myself, was a good start ! A few thousand dollars saved to put back into my reserve or to invest elsewhere in my business venture would come in very useful in the future.

After the initial success with the lot premium, I immediately switched negotiation to two other areas of this potential purchase. The first being the cost of the actual property itself, and the second being the furniture that I would need to buy to fully equip the house as a holiday home.

Firstly, in relation to the cost of the property itself, after more careful negotiation, I managed to get the cost reduced slightly, but this still represented a few thousand dollars. Every penny counted and this was another positive result. The savings were starting to mount up, but there was still something left to discuss, that being the furnishings.

Stop for a minute and just think about the things that you have in your home, which are not only essential, but what actually makes you feel comfortable and relaxed at home. Then, compare that with what you would need in a rental home. The list will include everything from the minutia of tea spoons, kettle and clocks to the more substantial items, such as televisions, beds, three piece suites and even a fully fitted kitchen, including all white goods. Your list will grow in no time at all.

The Americans are really big on white goods, and I mean big. They must have the biggest domestic refrigerators, dishwashers, washing machines and dryers in the world. They all look industrial size, but are terrific value for money and just what you need in a holiday home. Guests would certainly be impressed with those types of facilities, especially those on holiday with a young family. It would also mean that guests would need to take less clothing or other similar items with them, which in turn, would mean less luggage for them to carry. I would later learn that things, such as clothing, especially designer label clothes, jeans and electrical items, such as camera's etc, were so cheap to buy, that many people who travelled to Florida would travel out light and come back heavy !

They obviously took the opportunity to stock up whilst out there, but I am not sure how HM Customs and Revenue would view there spending spree when they returned to the UK. That would be a matter between the traveller and Customs as it would be for any other traveller from any other part of the world. This was also particularly relevant in relation to European countries, where bargains could be had by sharp eyed shoppers.

Now it came to the problem of furnishing the property and the associated costs of doing so. As it turned out, the developer had included the cost of furnishings within the initial purchase price. This was extremely unusual and this was the only developer known at that time, in that area, to have done so.

The furniture package was a significant package indeed. It included everything that I would need to get started, and I mean everything. This included all carpets, beds and bedding, all white goods, such as the washer and dryer, dishwasher, microwave, fridge/freezer and cooker. It even included a television, framed wall pictures and even enough cutlery and crockery for ten people, for both inside the house and the equivalent in plastic, obviously for safety reasons, for use around the swimming pool. Even though the property had four bedrooms, it would still be licensed to sleep ten people, hence enough of everything for ten !

It has to be said that taking into consideration the fact that the furniture package was included in the overall purchase price, I knew that the quality of the furnishings would be of a reasonable quality and standard, but it would certainly be no more than that. There were two options available to me. The first was to accept the furniture package that was included in the overall price, or alternatively I could try and negotiate to have the furniture package removed from the cost of the home and by using that money I could furnish it myself. The second option was possible, however, how realistic was it in terms of both my financial limitations and the time that it would take for me to shop around and purchase everything that I would need.

I settled on the fact that it was not practical for me to go alone to finance, find and purchase all of the items that I would need in such a package.

That was another decision made, but only one more thing to do in relation to that, and that was a final piece of negotiation. If I could save anything, anywhere, then it was worth doing. The realtors were probably getting a little bit fed up with me by now, but that's life and it was my money that was at stake and, with the exception of their sales commission, not theirs.

After all that, I managed to shave a few hundred dollars off the furniture package. I'm not sure if that was through skilful negotiation or through absolute desperation on the part of both realtors to get me to sign for a property and to get me out of there !

Overall, the day had gone very well. I had seen quite a lot in one day and even though I had intended to spend at least four days out of the seven looking around, I knew in my own mind that I liked what I had seen. My final shot to the realtors was that I wanted to basically reserve what we had agreed that day, and I would speak with them over the next couple of days after I had time to fully consider the whole deal. That presented no problem to them, with one exception. I would need to put a fully refundable deposit down on the lot that I had seen.

The deposit was $1,000.00 and as I did not normally carry that amount of cash with me, I asked if she would take a plastic card. The realtor said yes straight away, and took a swipe of my card for the refundable one thousand dollars.

To this day I still amaze myself and actually find it quite amusing about the fact that it is so easy to use a credit or debit card in this way to buy something so big ! It was only a thousand so no problem with that and my preferred lot was reserved.

I know that I had allowed four days to look around, but really, how much more was there for me to see? That evening, I drove around the developments that I had seen and even found one or two more, without my realtor being present. They all looked good and all had potential, all in the same price range, but none came up to the one that I had reserved. I even travelled around some of the more established estates to get a feel for how things develop. There were some fantastic properties located on estates overlooking some great golf courses. That type of property in those locations would certainly be an opportunity for me in the future. Everything about this whole business venture felt absolutely right.

I then took the opportunity to drive to another development which had almost been completed by the same construction company to view a fully finished model of the type of property I had reserved.

Later that night I returned to the town of Celebration and had something to eat in a lovely restaurant overlooking the lake. It was a great meal, a real good steak and a glass of red wine, sitting in terrific surroundings. Celebration is a place with what I can only describe as a warm, very welcoming and strangely enough, a homely feeling about it.

As a side issue and as I understand it, a short time after the development that I had seen opened up onto the market, the developer who as a matter of interest was one of the major construction companies in America, changed the furniture package facility and fell in line with other building companies in the area. The effect of that was furniture packages would still be available, but would be subject to either a cash or credit purchase or a separately financed agreement.

I had plenty to think about, however, the main decision in relation to committing myself to purchasing the property that I had reserved was already clear and my mind was made up.

The following morning, after an early breakfast around the pool, I decided to drive back to the estate and have a final look around. It was clearly going to be another scorching hot day, thankfully the air conditioning in the car was doing a good job.

When I arrived around 8am, there was a flurry of activity right across the development. There was a lot going on and to me it was apparent that this estate would flourish and be sold out in no time at all. To any potential buyer, who had the intention of buying property to rent out, my view was that this was an excellent overall package.

I left the estate and somehow ended up back at the town of Celebration. This would be the start of a very long love affair with a very beautiful place. I saw that there was a coffee shop named Barnies, which overlooked the lake. It was located at the end of the short street of very exquisite shops, near the Celebration Hotel.

I went in and although for many reasons I have never been a creature of habit, this would be the start of a routine that I would enjoy over many visits to Florida over many years. The instant, penetrating aroma of the vast array of freshly ground coffee beans and the accompanying mouth watering assorted American pastries first thing in the morning was a big enough hit to get those senses going, without actually taking the caffeine.

I had seen that there were some really nice wooden rocking chairs around the smooth, stepped concrete patio area at the edge of the lake. After buying a large coffee to go, I strolled over and sat in one of the rocking chairs. It was such a peaceful, relaxing and very stylish place to be. I would find it to be one of the places where I could sit and think things through very clearly and where, in time to come, as a result of my contemplations, I would make many very important decisions.

What a great morning, just after nine, clear blue sky and the sun was already beating down. What a start to the day and this would be a day that I would never forget. As I looked into the beautiful lake and saw some fantastic turtles, fish and even a very small alligator, I just found the whole place invigorating. This was what life was all about.

Whilst I sat there, somewhere in the background I could hear music, very soft music and then I realised, it was coming from a piped sound system that covered the whole area around the lake and shops. It was certainly not intrusive, it was actually very pleasant and very relaxing indeed. Everyone was so friendly and the whole place had a certain charm about it, which became almost like a magnet to me.

I was now so comfortable and completely satisfied that I had fully thought through every possible aspect in relation to this business venture and I knew that my mind was made up. Everything was in place and my business plan was clear in both my mind and on paper. I had even thought of a way that I could make a considerable amount of money on this new home before it was built. That will become clear as you read on !

I walked to the nearby public telephone, contacted my realtor and arranged to meet her back at the show house within the hour. Even that telephone call sparked another idea and another very easy way that I could and would make more money in the future !

As I drove out of Celebration, conforming to the 20 mph speed limit and observing the very pleasant motoring manners of the locals, which amounted to the 'after you sir, I'm in no rush' attitude, I was astounded by the type of houses that made up this incredible neighbourhood. All of the houses were of colonial design and they were simply magnificent. Beautiful homes with large verandas gently cooled by outside ceiling fans and overlooking very well manicured and quite extensive gardens. This was obviously a very wealthy area, and the cost of some of the properties must have been in the high hundreds of thousands of dollars going into the lower millions price bracket. I would later get to know some of the people who lived in that town and one of the most significant facts about those whom I did meet and get to know quite well was that they were predominantly self employed. This again confirmed my earlier thoughts that, generally, you don't get rich working for someone else. This town would become one of two places where I would find inspiration, especially when things became a little complicated or challenges had to be overcome. The other place could not have been more completely different, but it provided me with the same inspirational boost to my driving determination !

I took a slow drive back to the development, which was only about fifteen minutes away, and took another drive around the estate. I had no doubts whatsoever. Prior to travelling out to Florida, I was aware that I could possibly see so many properties that I would have difficulty in making a decision and I would end up not buying anything. As I had been totally realistic in my plans and very well researched, this did not present a problem to me at all. I knew what I wanted and I had found it.

The meeting with both realtors went well. It actually did not take very long at all to sign the necessary documentation and conclude that part of business, as we had agreed everything during our earlier negotiations and I had sufficient time to read and understand the small print !

The deposit was paid, and the only things that I had to do now were to complete and submit a mortgage application, open a bank account and choose what furnishings that I wanted for my new home.

The mortgage application was a very straight forward process, as I had all the required documents with me to show that I was a good financial risk. The local mortgage broker that I used had been recommended to me by someone that had used that company in the past to purchase their property in Florida. Once again, this was a very calculated decision to use that particular company, as word of mouth recommendation was much more reassuring to me.

The mortgage application, which again was an easy and very quick process, was accepted virtually immediately and I opened my new US Dollar bank account with a couple of hundred dollars. The bank was a local bank and had quite a number of foreign property owners as clients. The bank staff were used to dealing with foreign nationals who were operating short term rental property, and that again would make life easier for me.

With a mortgage in place, the whole process would now progress and I would need to have at least 20% of the purchase price of the property as a deposit, but it would not be required all at once. The procedure was that within approximately six to eight weeks, I would need to provide the first 10% of the overall 20% deposit, less the $1,000.00 dollars that I had already put down as the initial holding deposit. The remaining 10% of the deposit would not be required until the property was constructed and I would be required to pay that at 'Closing'. Straight forward I thought and it kept my money in my accounts where I could make interest over the nine months or so that it would take before the house was fully constructed. As I alluded to earlier, the construction time would be beneficial to my overall plan, allowing me to make money on the home during the building process which I could redirect to pay the remainder of the deposit as opposed to using my personal money up front. Once again, this will become clear !

My list of contacts was now building up. I had formed a very good relationship with both realtors, the mortgage broker and, as it turned out, with one of the business bankers at the local bank.

Some things never cease to amaze me, such as travelling well over 4,000 miles and going into a local bank where you hear an accent from your own area back in the UK. When I heard the northern accent, I just had to be friendly and say hello. The lady was one of the management team at the bank, and she explained that she had moved from my local area in the north of England to Florida many years ago. It would later transpire that we would build up an excellent business relationship and friendship over many years.

The final part of the purchase procedure was, as mentioned earlier, choosing a furniture package that I wanted for my new home. This would be my first real taste of the 'American Way' when it came to ease of buying goods ! I chose the colour and type of fitted kitchen, work bench tops, carpets, bathrooms and floor tiles with the realtor representing the developer.

For the remainder my realtor took me to a large warehouse a few miles south of the development to where I would meet a lady who represented the company that supplied all the furniture packages. It was another experience that I would not forget. The set up was such that lots of different rooms had been constructed and were on view inside the warehouse. The display included, amongst other things, living rooms, dining rooms, kitchens, bedrooms and bathrooms. There were many different styles, designs and colours of furnishings, and the enormity of choice was quite mind blowing at first.

I walked around for a while and selected what I liked and what I thought would be best suited for a holiday rental property. My decision in relation to colours of furniture was based on the fact that I did not want dark things in the house to make it look depressing, but I did not want something that would easily show marks or any stains. It was essential that the house had that instant wow factor as well as being warm, charming and homely. This had to balanced with being totally practical for me, the owner, to operate.

Being a man and the fact that, generally in my opinion, most men are renowned for not being very good at selecting furnishings, fabrics, colour schemes and associated domestic essentials, I decided to play it safe. I actually photographed everything that I had chosen, and just about everything else that was available, so my wife could look at the vast selection of goods and she could have the final say on whether we kept individual items or changed them for something else. This was a very good decision, and to my credit, after seeing the photographs, she only changed two or three very minor things. That piece of initiative really impressed her, and to be honest, I impressed myself with that one !

After choosing the furniture package, I returned to the development to take in things just that little bit more. I was extremely excited about my new purchase and I was trying to visualise how it would look. As I stood on the plot of land, it was then that I met another very good contact person indeed. The lady was a manager within the construction company, and she had specific responsibility for customer services and making sure that everything both inside and outside the new homes was absolutely right and that customers were happy !

Any problem with any thing, she was the person to contact. After I spoke with her and she had left, I thought to myself, what a lovely person, pleasant, professional and extremely focused on the needs of the customer. Exactly what I wanted and that was something that both her and I had in common. She wanted a happy customer and so did I !

It was at that point that one of the construction workers walked past me and made a throw away comment about the lady being able to turn milk sour at five hundred paces by just looking at it. When I asked what he meant by that, he said, if there were ever any problems and she was on the job, she basically put them through hell to make sure that whatever the problem was, that it was addressed immediately. All that she apparently understood was the word 'immediately'. Later was just not good enough for her or the customer for that matter. It did not matter how busy the builders were, when she said do it now, that's exactly when they did it – no questions asked !

That was the kind of person that I really did take a shine too and I could really get on with. Unknown to me at that time, I would require her services later, when a small problem did occur.

I added the lady to my list of contacts and made sure that her name was highlighted for future reference. My contact list was one very essential document. If I was to be over 4,000 miles away, I wanted as many contact details as possible. Those details included full names and company postal addresses, both landline and mobile telephone numbers, email addresses and any web site addresses, where applicable, of all the people that I had met. I also obtained contact details for their 'second in command' just in case the main contact person was not available. In this day and age of automative telephone answering services, nothing is more frustrating to me than listening to a very long winded computer recording of a droning voice going through a very long list of services and when you finally think that you have found what you want, the person is not available.

If you can, get their mobile telephone number and speak to the person direct. It saves a considerable amount of time and keeps your blood pressure down to a healthy level !

As you take in these experiences, once again, relate them to your particular circumstances. This process worked for me, and yes, I may have missed one or two things, or may have done them in a different way to some other people, however, at the end of the day, we are all different. This is a guide and it may greatly assist you, no matter where in the world that you buy your property.

One thought that I did have at that time was how easy the whole process had been. Predominantly, this was made easier by the very fact that there had been no language barriers involved. I wondered what would have happened if I had been buying property in a country where there had been a language barrier and how comfortable would I have been with the explanation about the documentation involved, especially the small print. As they say, the devil is often in the detail !

It was around 5pm when I got back to the villa where I was staying. I thought it best that I ring my wife to fully update her as to the days events.

She was very excited about what had happened and was immediately looking forward to the time when we could travel back to Florida together and see the finished article. There was, however, only one immediate issue to sort out back home and that was in relation to my car. My BMW motor car, which represented a large chunk of my deposit on the new house, was still sitting on the forecourt of a local dealership waiting to be sold. I had dropped it off there just before I flew out to Florida, that's how serious I was about realising my dream. My wife was ringing the garage on a daily basis to see if any progress had been made in relation to finding a buyer for it. Fortunately for me, the car would be sold within a few days and I could look forward to a nice little lump sum waiting for me when I returned to the UK. I had already seen another car which was for sale and would have to replace my BMW. It was a neighbour's old car, a Ford Fiesta with about 65,000 miles on the clock. It was basic, very basic, and it seemed to me that Fred Flinstones car was more luxurious than that !

However, it was one of those things and it had to be done. It was a set of wheels to get from A to B in, and that's all I would need for the time being. Think assets and financial liabilities I kept reminding myself.

Late afternoon, it was just the right time for a swim in the pool to relax after a busy day. It was still in the 90's and that was one of the main reasons why so many holiday makers, and particularly people from the UK flock to Florida in their vast numbers. This truly was the Sunshine State and just the weather alone made you feel really good. I started to think about how I would attract people into my property and how my business would be so different from so many others. The ideas of how to harness all of this potential income started to flow, even more so than when I had considered the same subject when I was in the UK. This was probably due to the fact that I had now actually seen some of the short term rental properties that would be my competition and I now had a feel for the whole thing.

Although I was very new to this, I could see straight away why I believed some owners were having problems in attracting guests to their property.

In my view, there was a secret to this, and as time moved merrily along, I would find that I would indeed crack the code to what I believe to be the mystery of success.

That evening I went to a restaurant that I had seen during my travels earlier that day. It was an Italian grill and was located just off Highway 192, near the area that was known as Splendid China. It had caught my eye as I drove past around lunch time. There was a queue of people outside the door who did not look at all like holiday makers, if you can stereotype and have such a thing. They appeared to be office workers and people in suits. As I arrived around 7pm, there was another queue of what appeared to be mainly families. From their accents and topics of conversation, it sounded like a vast majority of them were locals. If locals were eating there, well that was the sign of a good restaurant to me.

The meal that I had that evening was probably one of the best that I'd ever had. It was simply outstanding and this was another place that I would also visit on many occasions in the future. This was also a small, but very important part of my overall strategy to impress my guests with the high quality of service and information that I would supply to them. By being able to provide them with detail, such as where the best places are to eat out or to visit, goes along way to ensuring that they have one of the best holidays that they could ever have and they will remember you for it. Again, it is very difficult to beat personal recommendation.

I had done a lot of work in a very short space of time. The only immediate issue was that I had not employed the services of a management company, someone who would take care of my property whilst I was not there, although, through word of mouth recommendation from another villa owner, I did have a certain company in mind.

That would be a job for the following morning.

CHAPTER 7

Finding the right
property managers

I was fully aware from the very start of this venture that the whole future of a business concept of this nature would rest or fall on the three essential elements of firstly, successful advertising to secure guest bookings which in turn would generate income, secondly, providing an all round, first class, quality, prompt and professional service which in turn would enhance a good reputation, and finally, good property management which would ensure that my dream home would stay exactly that. This would be the very heart beat of my business and, in my opinion, for anyone considering entering into this particular area of financial investment, the importance of those three critical elements should never be underestimated or forgotten for even a single second. Without having those basic foundations in place, you will be building on sand, you will make life very difficult for yourself and cracks will start to appear in your lifelong dream. That is the last thing you need at any time, but especially at this stage.

If you have someone looking after your property who you consider is not totally reliable or if you have questions about their ethics, working practises, timeliness or honesty, you're going to have problems. They are going to cost you money, they are going to attract complaints from your guests, which in turn will gain you a poor reputation and cause you problems in the future in relation to firstly, dealing with those complaints and secondly, in the time it takes you to address those issues. My thoughts were that if you are dealing with issues of such a nature then your attention is being diverted from your main business aim of attracting guests to your property and generating income in the process. Therefore it's time to confine their services to the waste bin. Get rid is the simple and very clinical message and find someone who you can trust and who will do you a good job. You may say easier said than done, and that is true, to a certain extent. Do not be down hearted, believe me, it is possible as there are some good people out there !

Baring in mind that you are some considerable distance away from your holiday home, and in my case approximately 4,300 miles away, you can not just jump on an aeroplane and pop over to check things out anytime that you feel like it. Even holiday homes which are more localised, in European countries such as Spain or Portugal for example, with much less travelling time involved, can still present this problem. The people that you choose to look after your property are your overseas lifeline. You need to have someone who can be relied upon, who has high standards, will not rip you off and essentially, be an identified individual who will put your needs and that of your guests at the forefront of their minds. Overall, you need a good working relationship with them and this will go along way to receiving a good service with that all important personal touch. They are, in reality, an extension of you and your business.

You hear all about partnership and multi-agency working in this day and age and it is prevalent to all walks of life and all nature of business. If you have experienced, or are familiar with this partnership culture in your normal place of work, now relate those experiences, and the associated benefits to your own circumstances. The only difference being that, whatever you may have thought of such ideologies in your particular arena of work as an employee or as some form of stake holder, now relate that to your own business and you will see just how important it is. The reason that it is so incredibly important now is the simple fact that, firstly, it is you and your business that counts and secondly, it is another part of the overall strategy of ensuring that whatever you do will assist in putting money back into your pocket.

Property management played a large and very important part of my research before I purchased property abroad. After speaking with a considerable number of villa owners who owned property, not just in Florida, but in many other parts of the world, I heard various stories. The general consensus of opinion ranged from owners receiving a good or reasonable service to one which could only be described as being absolutely dreadful, and at times extremely 'questionable'.

If it were true, and I had no reason to doubt what some property owners had relayed to me about that particular issue, the things that some management companies or property managers told some home owners just to get their business, and their hands on other people's hard earned money, were alarming to say the least. Do not get me wrong, and it must be made clear, that not everyone can be tarred with the same brush. There are good people and bad people in every walk of life, it's just that the bad do cause real problems and, if this goes unnoticed, can ultimately lead to the downfall of some property owners.

This downfall may start, for example, with low quality or poor standards of service delivery from a property manager or property management company, which can lead to complaints from customers. One owner relayed an experience of where it developed into more extreme issues such as financial irregularities in relation to alleged services purported to have been supplied.

There are many examples of good property management and there are also many examples of bad. A common theme is that many new owners, who are possibly not as aware to the more sharp practises, fast talking or verbal promises of some, often find themselves in a situation where they believe that they have a good property manager or property management company taking care of their interests, but all may not be what it seems to be. It would appear that some of these managers or companies promise the property owner the world and reassure them about the quality of service that they will provide the owner. However, if there are any deficiencies in the provision of services, they will generally come to light in one of four ways. The first, being as a result of adverse comment or complaint from guests, secondly, from the owner themselves when they visit and see the low standard of maintenance or cleanliness of their property, thirdly, from other property owners with whom you can often build up a trust and good professional relationship with, and finally, when the property owner examines their monthly invoice from whoever may be taking care of their home, and they start to question the associated charges or fee's.

The issue of closely examining your monthly invoice or statement in relation to the management of your property is one of the most important aspects that can highlight any concerns, irregularities or be the initial indicator that all may not be what it seems.

Have your wits about you, scrutinise all of your monthly statements and never be afraid to ask questions. If you suspect something is not right, do something about it sooner rather than later and if that means terminating the services of those involved, so be it and do it before they siphon your money from your pocket into theirs.

The situation in relation to building up a relationship with other villa owners, particularly owners who have property close to your own, can be of great benefit. Briefly, the way it works is that whenever you go to your property, it just takes a few minutes to check out your friend's property to make sure everything looks as it should. If they have guests in at the time, then, even if you had keys or key code access to the property, you would not go inside for obvious reasons, unless pre arranged by the actual owner themselves with the guests. If you only get the chance to visit your holiday home once or twice a year, this allows periodic checks to be carried out by someone who you can trust. It is a form of spot check, which will give an overall picture of the standard of service that you are receiving.

One of the benefits of carrying out this form of impromptu spot check is that whoever is taking care of your property will not be aware that it is or has been done. Normally, the property owner will have to notify their property management company or property manager in advance of who is going to the property, their date of arrival and date of departure. The reason for this is due to the fact that every time you confirm a guest booking, you need to notify them to ensure that the necessary arrangements can be made to clean the property, for example, at the end of the guests stay or to make sure things such as food packs can be ready for your guests arrival or, if required, swimming pool heating can be switched on. Some companies also ask that they be made aware of when the owner is due to arrive. The reason that some give for this is, that they need to be made aware at all times of when the property will be inhabited for safety and security reasons.

The cynics amongst us, or the more experienced, which ever way you wish to look at it, may think that there could be a different reason altogether.

Could it be that it is only then that they make an effort to ensure that everything looks right for the time that they arrive. If so, what about the condition of the property the remainder of the time?

It is also not uncommon for a property owner, who on the spur of the moment and at a time when they have no guests staying there at the time, decides to ring his or her holiday home and very unexpectedly, someone answers the telephone ! Who are they and what are they doing there? Over the years, I have heard countless examples and accounts of this happening.

I could accept that, if the property was standing empty at a time when the property management company received a 'walk in enquiry', literally someone who goes into their office looking for holiday accommodation, and the company place that guest into your home, well it may not be a problem and the owner would probably welcome some additional, and unexpected, income.

The problem arises if this occurs and if the owner is not told about it. How much revenue is being generated by someone else out of the owner's property and without their knowledge?

This is an area that we will explore in detail and, as a direct result of such practises, one which went on to completely change my lifestyle altogether.

An additional benefit of building up such relationships with other home owners is in relation to the flow and exchange of useful information. It is amazing what you can learn about so many things, all of which are generally based upon other home owner's personal experiences. It is also another very useful way of finding ways to save money.

You will have noticed by now that I have made constant reference to the two different 'animals' of Property Management Companies and Property Managers.

I have done so for two specific reasons, firstly, so that you can identify that there are in fact two different descriptive names and types of service providers available, and secondly, that based upon experience and personal opinion, as far as I am concerned there are two completely different levels of service to go along with them.

Briefly, the differences between the two are as follows:

Property Management Companies (PMC's) are generally the larger type of organisation, who have a considerable number of properties registered with them. When I say a considerable number, it is not uncommon that this number could run into hundreds, all of which they endeavour to look after. As part of their portfolio of services to property owners, apart from the basic management functions such as making sure that the property is cleaned after guests leave, all bedding is washed, and the home is maintained to an acceptable standard, many PMC's may also offer other services such as, acting with your Power of Attorney and managing your escrow account, to pay your utility bills every month on your behalf or the placing of their own guest bookings, or even Tour Operator Bookings to supplement the owners self generated bookings. This is a very attractive way of enticing property owners to register with that particular PMC.

An escrow account is basically a sum of money held in your name and from which the Property Management Company pay your monthly bills when they are due for payment. You have to replenish your account each month to ensure that your pre agreed escrow balance is in place.

In my view, Property Managers have clear and very distinct differences to Property Management Companies.

The first thing to say about Property Managers is that, generally, they are normally the much smaller type of operation, whom have a much smaller number of properties registered with them. Some may only have a handful and others may have as many as around thirty or so. There is nothing prescriptive about the number of properties that they should, or should not, have. Over the years I have noticed that generally, these are either family run or man and wife, or some type of combination of alternative partnership working together. The result of this type of smaller organisation is, again in my view, that fewer homes should mean that a better all round service is delivered and that the all essential element of the personal touch should be a priority from the Property Managers.

Property Managers will also normally provide all of the services that you would need to ensure that everything in your home is taken care of, that everything looks right, all electrical goods are working correctly and that the property is maintained to a good standard. This would include the maintenance of your swimming pool and pool deck if you have one. It may be that some of the services that they offer are actually sub contracted out, and this may include for example, swimming pool cleaning and pool deck maintenance, carpet cleaning and lawn care or gardening services.

As with Property Management Companies, you will still receive your monthly invoice showing a breakdown and the associated costs incurred for your previous month, however, one of the main differences being that the PMC's may, at your request, be paying your utility bills, whereas many Property Managers may not provide that service.

In relation to the paying of bills, my view is that you should not allow anyone else to pay anything for you, unless you have very good reason, and even then, you must have absolute faith and trust in them. That is a particular issue which has created nightmares over the years for many owners and the reasons as to why will become very clear.

As I alluded to earlier, some of the most important aspects which I found in relation to differentiating between Property Management Companies and Property Managers were in relation to the level of personal service and the associated standards of service delivery that each one could provide.

As far as I am concerned, my own personal view is that out of all of the PMC's that I have looked at, they have definitely failed to deliver this important standard compared to Property Managers. If anything was going to be a clear and distinct advantage to my business, it would be the personal services that I could, and certainly would, offer to my guests, by identifying and employing an effective and professional property manager.

Unfortunately for me, at first and similar to so many other property owners, I experienced problems with a PMC. However, they say that every cloud has a silver lining, and that was certainly the case for me. As I gained more experience and became more confident in how to operate all aspects of my business, I started to get to know quite a number of people in both America and the United Kingdom. Over the years, as a result of this labyrinth of networking I was able to build up some very good, very diverse and very useful contacts indeed. It has to be said that some of these business contacts have actually become personal friends as the years have rolled by.

One gentleman that I got to know very well was working for a property management company when I first met him. I don't know about you, but I believe that I am a reasonable judge of character and the old adage of you never get a second chance to make a first impression always sticks in my mind. From the moment that I met this middle aged gentleman I got on with him like a house on fire. He was a genuine, kind hearted, intelligent and talented man who put his heart and soul into his work and overall he had one aim. That aim was to ensure that he did the best job that he could for anyone that he worked for and, in particular, he got a huge kick out of meeting guests at some of the homes that he maintained for a PMC. He actually loved to meet the guests at the villas as they arrived from the airport just so that he could open the front door of the property and show them inside. He just wanted to see their faces when they walked inside and saw the high standards of the property that he looked after. He would even hoover the carpets in a particular way so that it left an attractive pattern on the floor, and that's what I call attention to detail !

Again, just for the cynics out there, some may have thought that the reason that he did this and went out of his way to meet the guests was to try and increase his income by hopefully receiving tips from the guests. In all of the years that I have known him and after speaking with so many guests who have met him, I am not aware of any occasion when he accepted a tip from any guest. He did it for the buzz that he got from doing a great job. How rare is that in this day and age?

This to some might seem a little strange, however this was just the type of person that I really wanted to get to know as he had the same thoughts, feelings and standards as myself. Above all he was just a great guy who both my wife and I really got along with. As you will see, our business relationship and friendship developed and flourished over the years and all as a result of a chance meeting. Personally, I could see that he had a great opportunity to work for himself and provide such services and I had many conversations with him about that. He did not appear particularly happy working for such a large company and it looked to me like he was becoming disillusioned. Eventually he left the company and started his own, very successful business as a property manager. Personally, I think that it was the best move that he ever made as he was free to take care of the owners in his own, extremely professional way.

He greatly assisted me as I expanded the business and made sure that whilst I was in the UK the Florida side of my business was taken care of. Obviously at the first time of meeting him I had know idea that in the years to come I would receive so many letters, cards and e-mails from guests who booked holidays with me and whom had met my property manager. He really took good care of them and that's one of the reasons why people came back to me to book their holidays, year on year.

Think back and remember what I said earlier about creating a good reputation and providing a first class, quality service ! It is the heart beat of your business.

As a property owner, the whole aspect of Property Management Companies and how they endeavour to place guest bookings into privately owned holiday accommodation was one of great interest to me and one which you should be fully aware of. It must be stressed that not all PMC's are the same and not all have the same methods or working practices.

I mentioned earlier the term Tour Operator Bookings and this is an area which I feel should be expanded upon and one that you should be fully aware of. It can be a double edged sword, however, this again is an issue which you should fully explore if you are considering employing a Property Management Company to take care of your property.

After establishing the exact PMC operating procedures in relation to their general portfolio of standard services, one of the first issues to discuss with any potential PMC is that of Tour Operator Bookings and direct Property Management Company Guest Bookings. First of all you need to establish if they can provide that service and if so, what are the associated terms and conditions. As part of those terms and conditions, you should fully explore the rates that you can expect to receive from the PMC if they place a guest booking into your property, when will you receive that payment and exactly how the process will work?

From a personal point of view, whenever I heard a property management company say to property owners that they would guarantee so many weeks of guest bookings per year, my alarm bells started ringing, and ring very loudly indeed !

There were a number of issues surrounding that promise that really concerned me. Some of those issues being how can they guarantee a certain number of weeks per year of guest bookings, how many properties did they have registered with them whose owners had been told the very same thing, how much would the PMC pay the villa owner per booking, what would happen if they could not fulfil that promise and what could the property owner do about it if those bookings failed to materialise?

Would this be a contract between the PMC and the property owner and if so, how binding would that contract be?

Surely, if there was to be a contract the PMC would have included some kind of get out clause deep in the small print as I just could not see a way that anyone could guarantee anything, and my suspicions became absolutely true in the aftermath of those tragic events of 11th September 2001, when the number of visitors to the United States of America dropped immediately and dramatically. The tourist industry, especially in relation to visitors to Florida, was devastated for some considerable time after 9/11 and many private property owners 'went bust' during that period. The PMC's that I was aware of who had promised guaranteed guest bookings then immediately informed property owners that they could not guarantee anything in the future. My question was obviously, could they have ever guaranteed anything in the first place?

Maybe the cynic inside me said that it had been a good initial sales pitch by some PMC's to get the property owners on board with them, however the sales pitch had little or no substance behind it. What would have happened to any PMC with say two hundred properties registered with their company, could they have guaranteed the same thing to every property owner? So just where would have all of those guest bookings come from?

It is worthy at this stage to briefly explain the difference between a Tour Operator Booking and a PMC Booking. The two are obviously linked as they will both come from a PMC, however, the difference is that a Tour Operator Booking will generally be part of a pre-arranged agreement or contract that the PMC has in place as a result of negotiations with, for example, some of the larger travel companies or high street travel agent chains.

A PMC Booking may be, for example, as a result of an enquiry direct to the PMC from someone who is looking for holiday accommodation. A very good example of such an enquiry would be one that has been received by the PMC via their internet web site, or even someone who decides to pay an impromptu, spur of the moment visit and literally walks in off the street into the PMC office and enquires about the availability of holiday accommodation.

The double edged sword factor comes into play in the following way. In the initial stages of property ownership, especially when the property owner is 'brand new to the game', additional bookings, i.e. other than those that have been self generated, are generally very welcome indeed. In fact initially, many property owners do not mind at all as to where bookings come from, as long as they have someone paying them money to rent their property. It is almost a feel good factor that someone is paying them something, however, it is only later that many realise what the implications are. One of the main differences that they will soon realise is that when the property owner generates a booking for themselves, they will be able to generate significantly more income from that method. When they receive a booking from somewhere else, for example, a PMC, it must be borne in mind that other people are out to make money as well. As a result, others will endeavour to make money from the property owner in such circumstances. This was one of the most important factors that allowed me to change my lifestyle and one which you will see unfold as you read on. The whole principle of the property owner being the last person in the chain to make any money really troubled me, especially when it was their property that was being used or was accessible to others.

As a result, I turned the whole thing on its head and a business plan was formulated whereby the property owners would come first in the pecking order and not the Property Management Companies. I was only able to do this because of the strong foundations that had been put in place in the early days of the venture, which ensured that the guests who booked with me would have a great holiday. This was achievable due mainly to the high quality of service delivery combined with the attention to detail that I provided to customers.

If the property owner is fortunate to have someone who has sound business ethics and is professional in taking care of their home, they should receive a telephone call, e-mail or fax from them to inform them that someone is staying at the property. The owner should also be told how much they are going to receive from such bookings, and this should ideally be agreed at the very start when you enter into a contract with the property management company or property managers. The reason for this is again, based upon experience, you will otherwise have no idea whatsoever as to how much you will receive, or very importantly, when you will receive it. Once again, it is not uncommon for property owners who have experienced this, to have to wait months to receive payment, and when they do, it is an absolute pittance and is basically unacceptable. It may also be wise to clarify the method of such payment as you may find that the Property Management Company may not send you a cheque or pay the funds into your bank account, they may just credit your PMC account instead.

It was very clear to me to see what was happening. I could accept that if someone walked into the office and wanted to book there and then, not a problem. I could live with that, however, I was aware that some property management companies had Tour Operator Contracts in place. This was a completely different ball game altogether and one which I will now expand upon.

When the PMC's negotiate with the tour operators and large travel chains, it would be reasonable to believe that part of that negotiation and framework of any agreement would naturally include, for example, the estimated number of tourists that they predict over the following twelve months, the types, locations and standards of property that they could sell to their guests as part of a package and the associated pricing structure attached to that framework. The PMC's will be aware of how much income will be generated from Tour Operator Bookings and should therefore be in a position to inform property owners in advance, however, from what I have seen, it did not work like that. For some reason, some PMC's that I spoke with were reluctant to inform the property owner in advance of how much they would pay the owner for a Tour Operator Booking. Maybe, this was just some PMC's hedging their bets in case they could make more money out of the deal nearer the time and possibly at the property owner's expense.

One of the other issues in relation to Tour Operator Bookings is the fact that you have no idea who the guests are and how many people are actually in the party. The only time that I have known property owners obtain details of such guests is when the owner has telephoned their property and spoken with someone whom the PMC has placed in there.

I understand that the whole issue of securing bookings is absolutely essential to any business of this nature, whether it is the actual property owner or the PMC and it is almost like finding a golden goose if you tap into a good source which repeatedly produces guest bookings. I also understand that the source or any such golden goose is fiercely protected in order to maximise income, secure repeat bookings and to keep other PMC's and property owners away, however as the property owner, I would still want to know who was in my property, how many were in there and for exactly how long.

As the owner, if you personally generate and secure a guest booking you have had that personal contact with the guest and you know a lot more about them. As you gain more experience you seem to get that certain gut feeling and at times you can actually predict to a certain extent if that person were to confirm their booking and stay in your property, that you could encounter problems with them. An example of this being that I received a number of calls and e-mails from potential guests who were hoping to book with me, but when I delved into them a little deeper they were same sex parties, predominately male and every time it was some kind of celebration or a 'stag party' that they were going on. My view and my view only was, not a chance !

The only exception that I had in relation to same sex parties booking with me was in relation to a number of retired ladies and gentlemen who travelled out to Florida every year to play golf and small groups of businessmen who travelled out to Florida regularly and as part of their business they would spend time on the golf course. I had actually met with the lead person on occasions to take care of the arrangements and it was clear that they would not be a problem or a risk at all.

Some may find this approach a little strange, however, I had put so much into this business venture that I did not want anyone coming in and spoiling it by basically trashing my home or causing any other similar type of problem.

This again reverts back to the problem of PMC's placing guests into your home with whom you have no control over.

I know that some may take the view that if a PMC booking causes damage to your home that they should make good the damage or compensate you for the cost of that damage etc., however, that is not the point. That would certainly have a knock on effect to you and your business if the damage was so great and it would take time to sort out the mess.

As way of example, I knew of one owner who had a booking placed into his home for two nights only and it just so happened that included New Years Eve ! The booking consisted of a group of young men and women, and as I understand it some of whom were in their late teens.

Any alarm bells ringing yet !

You got it, they had what they thought was a great party and the house was very badly damaged, the cost of which to make good the repairs ran into thousands of dollars. It should never have happened, but it did.

It also took considerable time to complete the repairs, which in turn had that knock on effect as this prevented the owner placing any other guests into their home until everything had been taken care of. A real mess in more ways than one !

It must be said that not all PMC's or property managers are the same or have such practises, however, it is worthy of note just to be aware !

It goes without saying that the larger a business grows, the more work that is taken on, therefore the more staff that may be needed to make sure that all aspects of business is under-taken, to at least an acceptable standard or higher. As far as I am concerned, standards are everything, and in relation to my business, there has only ever been one standard, that being very high indeed.

One of the problems that I found and that has been high-lighted to me by other property owners is the fact that when a PMC grows, they sometimes seem reluctant to take on more staff to deal with the additional amount of work that goes with it. The effect of that is the quality of service and the personal attention that you will receive as the owner, may deteriorate.

In my view, at least with property managers, due to the much smaller number of properties registered with them, you have a much better chance of building up that rapport and personal touch whilst strengthening a very good working rela-tionship with them indeed. Regular contact with them, whether by e-mail or telephone, is essential for building up such a rela-tionship. E-mail is so easy, however, don't forget to pick up the telephone and speak with them. Get to know each other !

As you can see and as I mentioned at the beginning, the people who you entrust to take care of your property are in reality an extension of you and your business. You can also see how important it is to have the right people taking care of your interests. Choose carefully, ask around and speak with other property owners before you make your decision. Whether you choose a Property Management Company or alternatively Property Managers, is a matter for yourself, however bare in mind that you can not beat word of mouth recommendation !

Initially, I had a PMC looking after my property, but as time went by, I became dissatisfied with the service that I was receiving from that particular company and as previously mentioned, I moved to a Property Manager to take care of my interests. In my view, an excellent decision to leave that PMC.

CHAPTER 8

The Secrets of Success

'Set The Scene - Paint the Picture'

People find inspiration in many different ways and I feel certain that anyone who has that serious yearning for much more out of life constantly think about how they can achieve their goal. Some may already have the inspiration to do it and others may need a little help along the way. I was certainly one of those people who had the inspiration from the outset, but on occasions, a little boost did no harm whatsoever!

Apart from just generally thinking about how I could better myself, there were two special places that I would physically visit which I found to be inspirational and those places really did assist me in my thought process as I sat and planned my future.

Before I go into any detail, just remember, if you are one of those determined people and I mean committed and determined, and you want to achieve your dreams and goals, maybe you do something similar to me. It's not about the place where you may go to find inspiration or to think and plan your vision, really it's all about how you think and what you actually do about it that is crucial and critical to success. It just so happens that by going to these places it gave me an opportunity to set things out clearly in my mind and provided me with a motivational boost.

Many people have pipe dreams and talk about how they would like to be rich or what they would do if they won the lottery, but really when it boils down to it, what have they done about it and what are the odds of actually winning the lottery, especially if they don't even play the game? As they say, you've got to be in it to win it!

That equally applies to the desire for success. If you only talk about it and what you will do tomorrow, you'll get nowhere. For those who think that way, my view is that tomorrow never comes.

My change in outlook occurred many years ago and actually came as a result of my daytime job. There were a number of things that happened which totally changed the way that I thought about my future and about some of the people with whom I either worked with or became professionally involved.

As a result of what I did for a living, I saw many things that the public would never normally see, hear or ever come close to. As well as the excitement that went with my work and the places or locations that I worked in, I also saw on many occasions, both ends of the scale from extreme poverty to the very rich trappings of life. Whether it was the visible and very materialistic riches that I saw whilst looking after some of these people or the pure opulence of the places that they lived or stayed in, it made me think differently from some. As I pointed out earlier, I knew that I would never get rich doing my daytime job. It provided a relatively good income, travel and a decent lifestyle, but in that respect, I was no different to so many other people, except that I had this secret drive and determination to better myself. I looked at some people who were in business for themselves whom, and it has to be said, had been very successful indeed and I thought to myself if they can do it, why can't I?

In some respects I could clearly see that I possessed similar qualities to those people. The most obvious being that sheer driving determination and absolute commitment to succeed. The rewards were obvious, I just had to look at those people to see how they enjoyed a completely different lifestyle from so many other's and I just wanted to break out of the vicious circle that I was in. The vicious circle that I refer to has a vice like grip on most people and all they can do is work to pay the bills and hopefully have a little left over to finance some kind of enjoyment and limited lifestyle. I suppose that is the way of the world for most and many just accept that, but I really wanted to break free from what I saw as that everyday, life limiting, routine.

It certainly was not a case of looking on others with envy or jealousy of any kind, it was purely the thought of a complete change in what I was doing and actually controlling my own destiny.

If you have that certain drive to do things or you are looking to start afresh, you will know exactly what I mean.

I knew this had the potential to be big and I knew that I was committed. I also knew that there was no turning back. I just had to get this whole concept up and running as soon as I possibly could. People whom I had seen and who were very successful must have started somewhere, they had their ideas and they had succeeded, and I had mine.

At times, I just need to get away from people and go somewhere I can be left undisturbed, which allows me to think clearly. I would go to various places, whether it was for a walk around the village where I lived, a visit to a local coffee shop or even when I was out running and training hard to keep fit, I was always thinking about how I could take control of my future.

As I pointed out earlier, I did need a little inspirational boost at times, especially when things became a little challenging or when things did not go as I wanted them too. When that occurred, and on many other occasions I must add, I would go to what many would consider under the circumstances to be a strange place, and that was an area at a nearby international airport where all of the business men and women arrived in their privately owned or privately chartered jet aircraft.

Strange and why would you go to such a place you may say, however, I had good reason to go there. I found inspiration in the fact that when these private jets arrived, I would drink my coffee and look at the people who disembarked from the aircraft and the vehicles that would be waiting for them and this gave me a real sense of direction and something to aim for in life. Some people might think that it was literally pie in the sky or thinking well beyond my capability, but I did not.

I make no secret of it, who would not want a lifestyle like that? I was used to working in a very private and extremely discreet environment when I was doing my daytime job, and I had seen this over many years. The private jets, the beautiful cars, fantastic homes, how they travelled the world and how they 'did business' behind the scenes. I certainly wanted something better than I had in life at that time. I used to think, maybe one day, you just never know!

You may recall that I mentioned earlier the experience that I had in Florida the first time I visited the fabulous town of Celebration. That was the second place that I would go as often as I possibly could when I was on holiday or on business, to think and plan my future and to be honest, that was my favourite and a most very special place to be.

I was certainly an outward bound type and loved the outdoors. For years I had walked hills and mountains and witnessed some breathtakingly beautiful sights. However, for some reason, I found Celebration to be the most relaxing place that I had ever seen and the surroundings were quite exquisite. To this day I believe it was due to the fact that I could clearly distinguish between the two extremes of the hills and mountains being an internally satisfying place with those clearly beautiful views which made you feel better, and Celebration which had a different beauty, that of the sweet smell of success which provided such a fantastic outlook on life and the future.

Everything about that town just gave me the inspiration to succeed. You may have visited the town yourself and you may know what I mean, however, if you have not, then if you go on line and visit the town of Celebration web site you will get some idea as to what it is all about.

The whole point of mentioning inspiration is to prepare you for any challenging times ahead, and there will be some tough times. Few things in life come easily, and normally you only get the good breaks through a combination of thinking, planning, hard work and commitment. This whole process worked for me and it can work for you. So when the difficult times come along, don't get down hearted, regretful and negative, think positive and remember the reasons why you entered into the venture in the first place. Follow your dreams, but you have to work at it to succeed!

I firmly believe that there are 'secrets' which can lead to success and I also believe that, to a certain extent, I can almost predict with some degree of accuracy, the cycle that most property owners who encounter problems go through. This is based directly on my experience over the years that I have been involved in overseas property and in particular, the sheer number of property owners, and I mean a vast number, that I have known, spoken with, read or been told about.

There are hundreds of thousands of people in the UK who own a second home abroad and there must be millions of others who either seriously think about buying a property or have that dream of doing so one day.

The reasons why people purchase property abroad varies, however, it would appear that many just want the opportunity of owning a holiday home in a sunny climate to get away from it all and if they can generate additional income by renting their property out to guests, all the better.

Maybe some people think that the grass on the other side is always greener and when they commit to either moving abroad or buying a second home abroad, that's when reality sets in and things may not quite be as they always thought it would be.

The cycle that I have been mentioning is loosely as follows.

I have lost count of the people that I have spoken with over the years both in the UK and all around the world who own a second or even a third home abroad. Many have initially entered into the venture as an investment opportunity in relation to both the growth value of the property itself as house prices will hopefully rise and secondly, to generate income by letting the property on a short term rental basis to tourists. When speaking with so many of them, it struck me as to how little research some had actually carried out in relation to the logistics and commitment of operating such a property. Equally, the high expectations that some had that it would be a very easy investment as someone else could just look after the property on their behalf. It really is not as easy as just handing your property over to someone else to take care of it. That is a very simplistic view indeed. You could do that, but personally, I would certainly have reservations about it for many reasons. I suppose its everyone to their own, but what control would you have of your home, who would be making money from it, how much would you receive and what condition would it be left in? Just a few basic questions to open with and ponder upon!

Generally, as a result of what I have seen and heard over the years from so many property owners, particularly those who own property in Florida, the sequence of events can be broken down as follows:

1. The initial dream of property ownership.
2. The excitement of the actual purchase of a property.
3. Specifically in relation to new build properties, there is a perceived feeling of an 'abundance of time' on the part of the new owner before the property would be constructed and completed. The lack of logistical preparation and marketing activity from the owner between the time of initially seeing the development and signing to buy the property and the completion date, which in turn leaves them unprepared and not ready for business.
4. The 'honeymoon period' when they take possession of the home.
5. Attempting to rent the property to potential guests.
6. The disillusionment of being unable to attract paying guests, combined with competing against the large number of other properties available on the rental market.
7. The operating costs involved which is compounded by being unable to generate income from short term rental.
8. Subsequent loss of enthusiasm, self motivation and commitment to the venture.

9. The reality starts to sink in of what they have done and how much it has cost them.
10. Seeking advice in relation to selling the property.
11. The sale of the property and ultimate relief of selling up or foreclosure by the mortgage company or other lender.

Generally, and again in my view, that is the way that it normally works out for those who have encountered problems. To attach a time scale to it, well, anywhere between 12 to 36 months from purchase seems to be about the amount of time that it takes for some people to fall into this cycle. That is one of the main reasons why I have mentioned enthusiasm, commitment and inspiration so many times within this book.

You really have to work at it to get established and become successful and the second that you take your foot off the accelerator, that's when you are in danger of enrolling into that cycle.

I have seen this happen to so many people, so many times, that I have lost count of those who have gone through what can only be described as a horrible experience. The only relief coming to them is when they have actually got rid of their home abroad and their dream is, by that time, well and truly over.

Do not take what I have outlined as being just a doom and gloom view on life, it is not, it is reality. I have seen and heard it for years and I can actually see the early signs of it as it takes hold. It's not pleasant to see and I have tried to help a lot of people, but if they are not committed and the disillusionment has set in, it is very difficult.

Think back to the beginning of this book when I first said that there must be a secret to being successful and, one of the biggest questions of all being, what were all of those property owners doing that would cause them to fail in their venture and ultimately see their dream go down the pan?

Well, from the sequence of events that I have outlined, you can see just why this was happening. It was not unique to any one property owner or any particular property location, it was a common thread that was so apparent when I spoke with so many of them.

Use this as a positive guide, which will hopefully assist you to realise your dream and be successful while doing so. If you achieve that, hopefully you will also be very happy indeed with your overseas property.

I have now set the scene and, taking into account all of the factors that I have mentioned, this will again hopefully assist you in your decision making process to purchase the right property to fulfil your particular needs or requirements.

I will now paint the picture and outline some of the major factors that will again hopefully assist you on your way to success. This is based upon experience and they are all issues and areas which I considered as crucial.

As such, I put various mechanisms and systems in place which would ensure that everything that could be done was done to underpin the business concept and that the foundations were well and truly laid, enabling my business to make progress and grow. Some may seem a little obvious, yet so many owners have either not considered them, or if they have, they have discarded the issue as being either unimportant or unnecessary. Attention to detail in your initial preparation and all operating processes and procedures is a main key to success.

These are some of my 'secrets to success', they worked for me and put money in my pocket, so why should they not work for you?

At the very outset when you are thinking about buying property abroad, devise a strategy which will clearly identify that you are completely satisfied with the location of your venture, and I mean everything from the actual country itself to the location and even the site and position of the property. There may be several factors which will determine the country and location of your property, and that will usually be decided upon issues such as whether you want to let the property out to guests to generate income or, for instance, being in that very comfortable position of buying an overseas property for your exclusive use only. If you are entering into such a venture with a view to generating income, this process of elimination is essential. It is arguable to say that most people probably buy property based around the fact that they have been to a certain location before and they like the general area. If you base your purchase on that factor, be very cautious, as you may like the location yourself, but is it in the right area to attract sufficient paying guests?

As you may recall, I outlined earlier that I had never been to Florida in my life, yet ended up purchasing property there. That was based purely upon extensive market research and the prospect of future growth in all areas of the tourist industry, which in turn would greatly assist and feed my business.

The following will concentrate on issues that surround property that has been purchased, or is intended to be purchased, for the sole purpose of generating income from paying guests. It is important to fully consider the area of the market that you will be aiming to attract, in particular family based holidays, if that of course is your intention.

The size and design of your property will be a major factor and this will again probably be determined by your particular financial circumstances. As I have already outlined, I initially intended to purchase a three bedroom property, however, by taking a strategic approach to assist my decision making process, that allowed me to weigh up the positives and negatives every step of the way. As a result, I prevented myself from making what I believe would have been a big mistake at the very outset. That process allowed me to maximise my business opportunity, and very importantly, my income and ensured that I purchased the right size property, in the right place at the right price to fulfil my requirements.

The type of property that meets your specific needs is of course a personal choice, but again, put yourself in the shoes of your guests. What would attract them to rent your property, above all others that may be available on the market and what would ensure that they came back to you, year after year?

When choosing the best property for short term rental purposes, take into account the number of bathrooms that the property has for example. If the property is large enough to take eight to ten people, then additional bathrooms would be of great benefit, and a very good marketing and selling point, as guests do not like having to wait to take a shower or use the bathroom. My personal experience has shown that a four bedroom detached property, which has three bathrooms along with its own private swimming pool has always been a desirable property to let.

Additional attractive features which appeal to potential guests in a rental home may include, for example, a games room or a separate lounge where, if there are a number of children in the party, they can have their own space to entertain themselves, whilst still under the watchful eye and supervision of adults. That of course, allows the adults to have their space to maybe enjoy a meal or drink in relative peace and quiet!

The four main questions that I was invariably asked by just about every customer with whom I either spoke or corresponded with were:

1. How many bedrooms and bathrooms does the property have?
2. Does the property have its own private swimming pool?
3. How far is the property from any major tourist attractions?
4. Do you have any photographs of the property?

Virtually everyone asked those questions and you can see the importance of choosing the right property in the right location.

Again, based upon experience, I have no doubt whatsoever that a detached property with its own private swimming pool possesses by far the most appeal for tourists looking to rent private holiday accommodation.

As mentioned earlier, as a result of being in this business over many years, it was clear to see that a four bedroom detached property with three bathrooms and a private swimming pool was the most desirable property to rent and the easiest to sell to my customers.

If your resources allow, a Jacuzzi spa on the pool deck is a great selling feature as guests just seem to love lazing in a Jacuzzi, and who can blame them!

The demand for a private swimming pool is always high on the list of priorities for guests, and not only those with small families. It is clearly a very good selling feature indeed for property owners when marketing their property. The last essential element in relation to the issue of private swimming pools being available in private accommodation is the added facility of heating for the pool. There are generally three main types of heating for swimming pools, namely electric, gas and solar. Obviously if the pool is heated by electric or gas, there will be added costs to the owners expenditure, in particular their utility bills, therefore swimming pool heating is normally subject of an additional charge to any client. The cost of heating will vary depending upon the method of heating itself, combined with the size of the pool and even the time of the year, as some months will obviously be warmer than others.

Once you are completely satisfied that you have:

- Identified the right property for your needs
- You are satisfied that it is in the right location
- You have gone through the initial purchasing process there are a number of immediate actions that need to be completed. The actions can be broken down into areas such as:
- Property management, which I have already covered in some detail.
- Banking
- Marketing and advertising
- Administrative systems
- Communication
- Pricing structure
- and additional services to clients.

These may seem like huge tasks, however, once you start to look at the specific areas in detail, it is certainly not as daunting as it may first appear. If you deal with these issues straight away and identify how you are going to manage the different areas, then things will become very clear, organised and easier to see exactly where you are going with your business plan. I actually found it quite exciting to sit down and devise strategy, which would assist me to achieve my short, medium and long term goals. Ultimately, this was going to put more money in my pocket so no wonder I found it exciting!

Once again, I am convinced that this has been the downfall of many property owners and as I found out when speaking with them, their systems were not at all robust and some systems were almost non existent. It was apparent that some new owners did not cater for even the basics of what would be expected of them to operate such a business. I am not saying that you need large corporate systems or banks of computers in place to operate your business, however, I am saying that appropriate and robust systems should be in place, which are proportionate to your initial business plan.

Good administrative systems, attention to detail and forward planning are essential ingredients to help you along the road to success. I will go on to mention such systems in greater detail.

Before you leave the location where you have just bought your property, do not forget to deal with two critical areas. These areas are, as previously mentioned, banking and the preparation that is required for an immediate and effective marketing and advertising strategy.

If you have gone through the process of applying for a mortgage abroad, part of that process will probably be to open a bank account straight away in that particular country. Remember, I am basing this upon experience in Florida, however the process may well be similar in the country where you are considering buying your property.

When you open your bank account think ahead, in particular about how you will pay your monthly bills and take care of your finances. I found it beneficial to open an account with a bank that was in close proximity of my new home, which had experience of foreign property investors and could offer a very good personal service, as well as internet banking. This makes things much easier to control when you are at home, which could be thousands of miles away from your new acquisition. It also makes paying your monthly bills much easier if you set up the appropriate systems with the bank. The only other important issue that I would consider, again as a result of personal experience, would be to ensure that you have all the contact details of the bank and any personal or business banker. Remember much earlier, when I suggested that you keep a record of the names, addresses, telephone numbers, and e-mail addresses of everyone that you may need in the future, well this certainly fits into the category of very useful contacts.

With reference to marketing and advertising your property, at the earliest possible opportunity obtain as much information as you can which will aid your strategy in relation to attracting paying guests to your property. If you do not do this straight away and you forget to collect the information, you will put yourself in a very difficult position once you return home and start to think about how you will advertise the property. That is a general point that I feel that I should re-emphasise. If you have things to do which are clearly important to your business, the best policy is to do it straight away. If you don't, two things will invariably happen. The first being that you may completely forget to do it, and secondly, other important things will come along, which could be more urgent and take precedence. This in turn, will create a build up of work and take you more time to complete the tasks.

If you are purchasing a new property, gather as much documentation and information as you can from the developer in relation to the type of home that you have purchased and any special features of that particular development. The reason for this is that you will need to be able to show potential guests the layout of the property so they have a good idea of what they will be renting and this will assist in your sales technique. The purpose of obtaining information about any special features is so that you can tell potential guests about the area and use other things to help you secure bookings. An example of this could be if the development has a club house, communal swimming pool, tennis or volley ball courts, which are all attractive features and may really assist the client to make the decision to rent your property as opposed to any other.

When you are considering what information you will need to assist in your marketing and advertising strategy, look at it from the points of view of both the owner and potential guests. As the owner, you have just purchased your dream property and that is exactly the way that you need to market and advertise it. As a potential guest, think about what would attract you to renting that particular property above all others that are available on the market.

Probably the most important factor in relation to marketing and advertising is images of your property. Without well thought out, clear, attractive and impactive images, you will be disadvantaged and will not put yourself in a strong position ahead of other competing property owners.

Over the years I have seen many images of property being advertised in various ways and, on so many occasions, the poor quality of some of those images never ceases to amaze me. Taking into account, the whole concept of such a business is to attract guests who in turn will pay you money to rent your property, it is clear that some owners leave a lot to be desired in relation to this critical element of their plan!

I am actually being very kind when I mention the words 'their plan', as it is clear to me that some appear to have little or no idea whatsoever about how to attract guests and some of the images that I have seen can only be described as utterly unattractive, poorly thought out, and generally appalling. You may consider these to be strong words, however, if you are going to put yourself into this type of business, you have to give yourself a sporting chance of success and create as many opportunities and advantages over the opposition as possible.

As a paying guest, if I was looking to rent holiday accommodation I would first of all take a real good look around to see for myself what was available in terms of location, quality and price. Personally, I would start by searching the internet, and I cannot stress the extreme importance of that marvellous world wide tool for a business of this nature. One of the first things that would attract my eye to advertised holiday accommodation would be the quality of the images which in turn would clearly show the type of property being marketed.

I have been very successful indeed in attracting guests to private holiday accommodation over the years and this is down to a number of things. Firstly, attention to detail is so important and this is surely the foundation of all aspects of any successful business. Secondly, confident sales technique, thirdly, providing the customer with a first class, quality, prompt and professional service tailored to meet their individual needs and requirements and lastly, by using as many visual aids as possible to clinch the sale. Obviously, as part of the visual aid approach, it will include images of both inside and outside of the property as well as documents such as floor plans and maps of the area, which build up the information package and a clear picture for the client.

I take the view that the images an owner chooses to advertise and illustrate their property can make or break them, especially, if they are totally reliant upon paying guests to pay their mortgage and everything else that goes with owning property abroad. To get the best out of your marketing and advertising strategy, start with good quality images of your property. I have found that a combination of shots showing both external and internal features, fixtures and fittings attracts viewing straight away from potential guests and leads to enquiries, which in turn can lead to confirmed bookings and ultimately, money in your pocket.

Starting with the outside of your property, look for the best angle that will show the front of your home and choose a sunny day to capture those images. Pay particular attention not to include any shadows that may be cast as that will not only darken down the image, but darken down the interest and enthusiasm of potential guests. You may think this to be a little finicky, however, I know what people look for and I also know what not only attracts their attention, but holds it as well. I am also very much aware of what will turn them away to someone else.

When you are looking for the perfect image of your property, as I have mentioned, pay particular attention to the type of day it is and the weather conditions at the time when you are about to capture the images. For example, I have lost count of the images of property that I have either seen being advertised generally, or the images that have been sent to me by owners, which clearly show the property, but they have been taken on a stormy day where the sky is dark, almost black in some cases, and the road or footpath outside of their home is covered in water showing that it has been raining.

These are not the type of photographs that are going to assist you in renting out your home. When I think about taking a holiday, I picture blue sky and sun not stormy skies and rain and I'm sure that many others think the same!

Don't put your customers off, go for the feel good factor from the start.

Once you are satisfied that you have some good, clear, bright images of the front of your property, start thinking about images of the swimming pool if you have one. If there is also a communal pool, think about including that in your image package. I do not profess at all to be a good photographer, but I know what is attractive to guests and what sells the property. I have seen many images of swimming pools, and once again, considering that is one of the best features of the home and one of the best selling images in relation to private accommodation, you would be amazed at the poor quality of some of those images.

Once again, so many images show poor weather conditions in the background, or dark shadows cast over the pool deck area. Many images are poorly captured and only show half of the pool, which does absolutely nothing to stimulate the interest of potential guests. I have also seen countless images which clearly show building and construction work taking place in the background. Any construction work taking place, even if it is in the distance and does not actually effect your property, can create concern for guests and people do not want to see that. It can lead to guests bypassing you immediately and moving on to other available property. If there is any construction work taking place which would effect their holiday, it is only right that you tell them about it and let them make informed decisions. This will prevent any possibility of attracting complaints from guests whilst the work is ongoing and protects your reputation. However, if the construction work is so far away that it does not affect either your home or the quality of a guests holiday, why include it in the image as firstly you are only creating a problem which does not really exist and, secondly, the construction work taking place will progress and hopefully it will be completed in a timely fashion. The problem that you would encounter then is that you would need to obtain new images as your original ones would still show building work, which over time, would have been completed.

As I have said many times, guests want to see blue skies and the clean, clear sparkling water in the swimming pool, which looks so inviting that they just want to jump in. The pool deck area is a great feature to illustrate and as such, try and maximise its effect on your property. Guests really like to see how big the deck area is in comparison to the swimming pool. Generally, they also like to see the sun lounges around the pool deck area that they will be lying on topping up their sun tan!

I find that both a daytime shot and an image in the dark with the underwater pool lighting and subtle pool deck lighting illuminated creates the right ambience and a very good effect on the eye, and again maximises the opportunity to attract guests.

Now that you have the external images of your property, start thinking about the internal shots which are going to really impress guests. One of the better ways that I have seen to create the right impression is to capture images of going in through the front door to create that immediate wow factor.

Once inside, carefully select the best angle to get as much in as possible. I have seen some particularly good images taken from height, where the owner has used a step ladder or something similar to stand on to get that little bit more out of the shot. Generally, the internal images should capture the living room(s), dining area(s) and kitchen in order that the guests can get a good and, once again, immediate feel for the property. Try and use any internal lighting, such as table lamps, to create that warm, homely and inviting feeling. Try to avoid closing curtains or blinds as that really closes down the image.

Sleeping and bathroom arrangements are the other essential features that guests will always need to know about. If, for example, you have a master bedroom with en-suite, then use that to the maximum effect. The images should again be warm, homely, clear and show the high standards of cleanliness of your property. Maximise your shots of the other bedrooms and any other bathrooms that you may have. How many words does a picture paint?

Once you are satisfied that you have captured the best possible images of your home, and that you have a good selection to choose from at the moment and to refresh your advertising in the future, apply your thoughts to how you are going to arrange the images to attract maximum attention.

There are many ways of doing this and again, it is personal choice. However, as the intention is to immediately attract and hold the attention of anyone browsing the vast number of holiday homes available, you need to have your most impactive images right in front of their eyes.

It may be difficult to have more than one image that appears when, for example, someone is doing a general search on the internet, and they may have to enter your particular site to view further images. Therefore, you need to decide whether you are going to have a great shot of the front of your property that is immediately visible to the browser or maybe, for example, a great image of the swimming pool at night. The choice is yours and you can always change the images periodically.

At this point it may be worth mentioning that if you change something about the way that you advertise, make a note of what you have been doing, what you have changed, how you have changed it, and what are the outcomes? Monitor and make comparisons all along the way in order to try and gauge the success of your decision making process and advertising strategy. This forms part of your market research which I found so incredibly important and can guide you in the right direction. It will also keep your advertising costs to the minimum, whilst hopefully maximising your income. If you have that structure in place, it is certainly more scientific and economic as opposed to a constant shotgun blast approach to expensive, and often unproductive, advertising.

When arranging your images I personally favour one of the front of the property and one of the swimming pool right alongside one another. That has always seemed to capture enough interest for the potential guests to delve in a little deeper and look a little further at what I had on offer and available to them.

Once you have illustrated the front and rear, try to arrange the internal images as you would if you were to walk through the property. The reason for this is that the client may want to compare those images with the floor plan of your home, which shows where everything is located and even dimensions of rooms. Believe me, it is amazing what questions many guests have in relation to property, especially those who are organising a holiday for a number of people, such as two families. Their reward for taking care of the arrangements is normally to choose, what they see as, the best bedroom to stay in once they arrive at your home.

I will go on to outline some of the successful ways that I have marketed property over the years and how text falls in alongside images to give that easy on the eye and easy to read format, which holds peoples attention and prevents boredom or frustration setting in.

One issue which may cause some problem for you is if the property that you have purchased is a new build and yet to be constructed. That was the position that I encountered when I first started out. One way of dealing with it is to find a model or show home property, on the same development if possible, which is similar in every way to your new home. Take as many photographs of it as you need to ensure that you have covered all of the angles and that you have a broad assortment to choose from and use them until you can obtain images of your property when it is completed.

It's not ideal, however, this will put you in a position where you can prepare and advertise without undue delay. The only thing to add is the fact that, when I had to do this, I actually informed all guests and potential guests that the images that they had seen were similar in every way to that of the property that I had purchased.

I never had any problems at all doing that, and many people actually thanked me for my honesty and integrity.

As I have mentioned previously, take your time and pay attention to detail especially when you are in the process of capturing images of your property. To refer once again to that well known cliché, 'you never get a second chance to make a first impression', generally that is very true in this line of business as the images that a client will view in the first few seconds will go along way toward making up their mind to choose your property.

Don't forget, before you leave to return home after purchasing your new property, obtain as many images as you can of your new acquisition, or one which is very similar in every respect, to assist launching your advertising campaign. Also, don't forget about images of any special features such as tennis and volley ball courts, any clubhouse or communal pool and anything else, such as communal play areas for children that could make your property more appealing than any other on the market.

Do not wait until later to think about it as firstly, you will have wasted valuable time by being unable to advertise and attract guests, and secondly, unless you can return to the location of your new home yourself, you will have to contact other people and rely upon them to obtain images on your behalf. If you do that, you can bet that they will probably not pay as much attention to that task as you would like and they would probably not capture the images that you want. Remember, it is your property, your venture and you have to make it work for you from the start.

To sum up this issue of images of your property, everything you do in relation to marketing and advertising your property should scream out to potential guests **"YOU WANT TO RENT THIS HOLIDAY HOME"**!

Whatever type of property that you purchase, whether it is new or re-sale, when you return home after the initial purchase, do not waste any time at all and get straight into setting up your systems, including implementing your marketing and advertising strategy.

Generally, you may find yourself in one of two situations, either one of which will have different time scales involved in relation to taking possession of the property and before guests can actually spend time there.

Firstly, if you purchase a re-sale property or even a brand new property which is constructed and complete, the time that it will take for the purchase process to run its course before guests can actually visit the premises will obviously differ considerably to that of a new build property which has yet to be constructed. I found that the time scale involved in my new build property after signing and paying the initial deposit took approximately ten months from start to completion. Other properties in other locations may take much longer and that is an issue which you will need to discuss with the developer in order to identify any target date for completion.

Dealing firstly with resale property or a new property, which is already constructed and 'ready to go'. The time that the new owner will have in these circumstances, before they take full possession of it, may well be measured in just a few weeks. That will also mean that in a very short space of time, they will be responsible for all the running costs of the home, including any mortgage payments that they may have. That, in effect, puts pressure on the owner straight away, as unless they can afford to operate their new home without having to rely on income from guests, they will need to find sufficient funds to cover the monthly expenditure.

In Florida, part of the purchasing process in relation to the mortgage application included showing that you had the first six months worth of mortgage payments 'up front', however, that may differ in other countries. The benefit of that process being, you would have a safety net for the first part of the year, which would buy time for you to attract paying guests to your home. The downside is, however, and as way of caution do not let the fact that you have the first six months mortgage payments covered effect how and when you launch and advertise your business. Time is critical at this stage and your business should be ready to go. The worst thing that you could probably do at this stage is to be lured into a false sense of security, sit back and think that time is on your side, as before you know it, six months will have flown past and you could end up in a situation where you will immediately have difficulty in finding sufficient funds to cover your monthly expenditure thereafter.

On the other hand, if the property is a new build and yet to be constructed, you will have a reasonable amount of time before you would actually take possession of it and before you start paying the associated operating costs.

I have already mentioned that, in my case, it took approximately ten months for the property to be constructed and completed. In addition, I did not take actual possession of it until about one month after that, and then it was another month after that before I had to make my first mortgage payment. In effect, I had twelve months between initially signing for the property and paying the deposit to paying my first mortgage payment after completion.

As you will see, that was an opportunity that I really exploited and you can now see the difference in financial time scales between re-sale/ready constructed and new build property.

Even though there are different critical time scales involved, the principles remain the same. If you want to be successful and make money you have to work hard, put the hours in to get the business off the ground and that work starts straight away. I can not emphasise enough, do not delay!

You have to make sacrifices, and yes, there will be times when you may want to do something else, or would rather be with someone else, but do not let anything or anyone distract you. Your destiny is in your hands so make it work. Use your drive and determination, throw yourself into the business and your commitment will soon start to reap the rewards.

As soon as you return home, start putting everything into action. Your preparation is essential at this point and I find that, no matter what I am doing, I need to be organised and have systems in place so I can see exactly what needs to be done and where I am going. I find that by being organised and having a suitable place to work, in private, ensures that I prioritise everything, nothing gets missed and the work is completed either on time or ahead of schedule. That way of thinking had been instilled into me on my first ever day in my daytime job and it was something that I would never forget.

You may recall that I mentioned earlier that even before I travelled to Florida I had prepared certain things which would once again ensure that my business would be ready to go as soon as I returned. As part of that preparation, I had converted the smallest bedroom in my home into my new office from where I would be able to operate the business. This to me was a very important decision as it allowed me to work in private, in a suitable environment where I would not be disturbed and everything that I needed would be at my fingertips. I wanted to create a professional and corporate image for both myself and the business from the very start and for me that was the right way of doing it. As you will see, creating and being in the right environment would become particularly significant when I started to speak with clients on the telephone.

I started with a decent desk which was large enough for me to work on and have my desk top computer and printer at hand. Along with that, I invested in a comfortable chair, as I knew that I would spend many hours at the desk, and I did not want to end up with a bad back. I also did not want to be distracted from the business at hand through an uncomfortable seat!

I distinctly remember the excitement that I experienced when I returned home. I arrived at Manchester Airport around 6.00am, drove straight home and managed to get a few hours sleep after the overnight flight. All that I could think about was getting on with the business and by late morning I was up and well into completing the final preparation of my advertising material.

I had already prepared basic templates before I had travelled to Florida and to start with I needed a number of things in place. The main areas that I had concentrated on were firstly, I had to be ready and in a position to immediately provide both verbal and written information to customers upon request. The written material would be in the form of a basic, but attractive, 'brochure'. Secondly, I needed to advertise the fact that I had property available for short term rental in Florida in order to attract enquiries. That, initially, would be in the form of word of mouth from me to anyone that would listen and flyers which I put up on just about every notice board in every building that I went into. In the early days I always had my 'advertising pack', which basically consisted of lots of flyers and brochures with me in the car. The reason for that was it was free advertising and would keep costs down to start with. With my business head on, I always looked at everyone that I knew or met from the point of view that they were a potential customer who could put their money into my pocket. As I said before, never ever miss an opportunity!

To advertise first and then think about preparing the information to send out would have created problems as it was pointless advertising if I could not provide immediate information to customers. I always knew that I would have to 'strike whilst the iron was hot' and that meant if a customer asked for information it would be prepared immediately and sent to them either by e-mail or post without any delay whatsoever. If I delayed providing the information, even just for a day, that could mean the client losing interest in me and my business. I could have been seen as unreliable which would cause the customer some concern and ultimately the customer would go to another property owner, which was the last thing that I wanted. A vast majority of the information which I sent to clients once I had received their initial enquiry was sent, wherever possible, within the hour and that prompt service was often the subject of very favourable comment indeed from customers.

As part of my research before I travelled to Florida, I had contacted many holiday home owners and asked them to send me any information that they had in relation to their property so that I could have a good look at what may be available as a possible place for me to stay when I travelled out there. To be perfectly honest about it, the first thing I noticed was that so many of them did not ask me about anything in any great detail. In fact, I was unable to speak with a lot of owners and all that I could do was either leave a message on their answer machine or send them an e-mail requesting that they send me anything they had. Some responded, however, many did not and that was a startling message in itself. For all that they knew, I was a potential customer who may have wanted to rent their property year after year and in reality give them money, but it appeared that they could not even be bothered to return my call or send me an e-mail.

I have always been careful not to do anything that could be seen as underhand and I certainly would not do anything unlawful, but I did create advantages for myself whenever and wherever possible. I also saw that a spin off from my enquiries to owners was a form of market research and it would not, for example, create copyright or plagiarism issues. Apart from looking for somewhere to stay, I also wanted to actually see what kind of service the owners would be providing to me as a potential customer and what quality of information they were sending out. I also wanted to know how I could improve the service that I would be providing and it soon became clear to me that many owners were falling at the first hurdle by sending out very poor quality and extremely unattractive information packs to potential guests. When I say information pack, in relation to some, I use that term very lightly and very loosely indeed as many were nothing more than a sheet or two of paper. Some were nothing more than black and white, grainy images of a building which would have certainly put me off renting straight away.

The cross section of information that I had received was literally from one extreme to the other. Some could only be described as totally unprofessional, unattractive and a certain way of turning potential custom away, yet others were very good indeed and you could see that a lot of thought had gone into their work.

The better ones were well presented, structured, and very attractive on the eye with a good balance of images and text. Most had terms and conditions attached and some kind of booking form to complete. Generally, everything was there but I could see room for improvement.

My initial information pack, or 'Pack A' as I termed it, would be the package that I would send out immediately to any potential customer upon receipt of their enquiry. It consisted of a number of pages in A4 size, which immediately and clearly illustrated what the property looked like, a full description of the property itself, where it was, and a breakdown of what services I had available to customers. It was produced in colour, it was attractive and very easy on the eye with sufficient text to describe the property and inform in every detail, but not too much, which could have looked cluttered or created boredom. It also included information in relation to special features such as the clubhouse, communal swimming pool, tennis courts and children's play area. In addition, there was a feature on the theme parks and other major tourist attractions, good restaurants and other places to dine out, specialist discount and designer outlets and all of the major shopping malls and local supermarkets. It also included the distance to such places from my property and associated travelling time by road. At the end of the pack, I had included the price structure for different times of the year, a booking form and a copy of the terms and conditions. Every time that I sent a pack to a customer, it also included a covering letter which was intended to ensure that the customer knew they were getting a very personal and specifically tailored service to meet their needs. I wanted each and every customer to know that they were special to me and that they were getting a first class, professional service. It was, what I believed to be, a well rounded and very informative document, which was extremely user friendly.

The detail on every page was very important, however, the first page had to be so impactive that it would reach out and grab the customer's attention straight away. That is why it is so important to take the time to obtain good, well thought out images of your property. It really is essential to make sure that your property looks at its very best, all of the time, for any potential customer.

As soon as they saw the property when they opened the hand written envelope or the e-mail, it had to give off that wow factor and as they perused the other pages and saw the high quality images of the inside and the swimming pool area, it really had to hook them!

The 'Pack A' worked hand in glove with my honest, open, and very friendly sales technique and this ensured that, unless the enquirer specifically outlined that they only wanted to be contacted by e-mail, I had the opportunity to speak with customers and sell my product over the telephone. It was a basic, yet extremely effective sales technique which worked very well for me.

You may have noted that I mentioned hand written envelopes. This was another deliberate tactic to let the customer know that I was giving them my personal attention and that they were very special to me. Computer generated names and addresses on envelopes may look very neat, but they are very impersonal and could, on occasions, be mistaken for junk mail.

I knew that I would also need a further document, which I termed my 'Pack B', and that would be the final travel information pack that the customer would receive once they had confirmed the booking with me. That document was a priority and was well on its way to completion, but I knew that I had a little more time to perfect it as my new home would not be ready for approximately ten months and the customers would receive the Pack B from me eight weeks before their date of arrival at the villa.

Advertising is an absolutely essential ingredient to make your business a success and as I have mentioned, I initially and immediately started distributing flyers and brochures to friends and colleagues. On the first day that I returned from Florida, I had a friend contact me and asked if I had bought a property. I told him that I had, described it to him and when it would be ready and he made a provisional booking straight away, which he later confirmed. That was my first sales pitch and my first confirmed booking was for the Easter holidays after the completion date.

That was the very first day, the very first booking and the start of many more to come.

My research had shown that advertising could be extremely expensive, so I really had to think about how I was going to get my message out there. I looked at so many adverts for holiday property abroad to get the feel for things and to check out the competition and their prices, that I lost count of the number that I had seen. What struck me was the sheer number of small adverts all lumped together in the middle to back pages of newspapers or magazines. They probably cost a small fortune, for a few lines, in a publication where your advert would be like trying to find a needle in a haystack amongst all the others. It did not make sense to me to spend all that money on advertising that was basically a lottery as to whether it would ever be seen, never mind yield any results. I wanted to concentrate on more 'target specific' audiences and, in particular, areas where my costs would be kept to the absolute minimum.

I started by using the intranet system at my place of work and a local internal publication to start to get my name known. It was free of charge and would be circulated to thousands of people. At the same time, I contacted other organisations in a similar field to where I worked and I was able to advertise on their systems and internal publications, again, free of charge. All that I did was include in my advert the fact that I would be in a position to offer a discount on the price of renting my property to employees of that particular organisation. As it happened, I had already devised a price structure which incorporated the fact that, at times, I would need to be in a position to offer 'mates rates' as opposed to that of complete strangers. This is another area that I will expand upon.

Before I knew it, after applying some thought to my strategy both before I travelled to Florida and after I returned, I was soon advertising to a large number of organisations around the UK which had an overall audience of hundreds of thousands of people. I contacted countless large organisations and companies all over the place and yes it took time to speak with people and at times, negotiate how I would be able to obtain free advertising, but overall it was extremely successful.

If you think of day to day products that you use or places, such as supermarket chains, where you may visit and how many employees those companies have on a national or even an international basis, you start to get a feel for how many people you can reach out to and all for the sake of a telephone call, followed up by e-mailing your advert to the companies for publication. That was an example of general advertising, but as I mentioned earlier, try and be more target specific and direct your advertising and energy toward people that you know visit the place where your property is located.

An example of such targeting for the Florida market is that every year, you see shows and performances taking place with a Florida related theme. Thousands of people visit such shows. For the sake of printing two or three thousand flyers and obtaining permission to distribute them at the various performances, that is very target specific. It is directed toward people that have made the effort to come and see the production so maybe they have more than just a passing interest in the show and Florida may well be the destination of their next holiday. If you are fortunate, you may be able to negotiate some kind of advertising deal to erect a display or some other similar facility within the building where you could really attract the attention of so many people within the audience.

One of my methods of advertising served two purposes. The method was simple enough, just identifying appropriate large housing estates and posting flyers through letter boxes. Not very original, not very scientific and not really target specific you may say, however, that method did reap success and at the same time was a great form of exercise. It got me out into the fresh air, but at the same time, I was still working directly on the business and it allowed me to think as I walked around about what I would do next to grow the business.

When you think about the whole process of what you are doing as a property owner, all you have to do is attract enough people to fill your available dates and you can only fill so many weeks in any one year. Baring in mind that you will probably be visiting your holiday property more than once a year, you might only have a maximum of approximately 46 - 48 weeks in any year available. It may initially seem like a lot of weeks to fill, but when you think that many people will spend two or even three weeks there, those available dates soon diminish. The problem is attracting guests to your property and getting them to come back to you in future years. I firmly believe that the best form of advertising is word of mouth recommendation and that was my intention from the start. By offering a totally professional and personal service tailored to individual customers needs, that is how I managed to build the business and attract so many paying guests to both my property, and many other properties, as the business grew.

It's all about opening up the mind, applying some thought about how you can either obtain free advertising or 'piggy back' on someone else. An example of 'piggy backing' would be negotiating a deal with local travel agents to use your property for their guests or recommending a particular travel company to guests when they are looking to book flights and in return, the travel company would recommend you to some of their customers. Try to use the corporate spending power of some of the larger organisations to aid and carry your business along.

Never be afraid to go and knock on someone's door if you need something. If you have a particular problem, find out who can help and go and see them. They can only say no and refuse to speak with you, however, they may just be in a position to assist you. I have been in that predicament before and I have researched the problem and identified who could possibly help me, such as local government offices, banks, major travel companies, hotels for discounted deals for use of their corporate exhibition facilities etc. and I have never hesitated on either making an appointment to see someone, or if that presented some kind of problem, go and knock on their door. It is amazing what help is out there if you go and look for it. If you have any reservations about doing that, just remember, what you are doing is for you, your business and you're future.

If you need to overcome a problem or you need some kind of assistance and someone says no to you, just persevere until you find the person who can and will help you to get the answer.

As a result of piggybacking on someone else, this will ensure that your costs are kept to the absolute minimum whilst gaining maximum personal benefit. Those benefits can be in one of two forms, either financial or alternatively, through networking and making new contacts, which in turn may open new doors for the future.

I always noted that every time an advert appeared on either television or radio which advertised the magic of Walt Disney

World, Florida, that in itself was indirect free advertising for my business. It appeared that every time the adverts were aired, which seemed to reach its peak immediately after the Christmas and New Year festive holiday period, I received more and more enquiries from people who were spurred on to arrange a holiday in sunny Florida. There just had to be a correlation between those adverts and the increase in the amount of enquiries that I received. As my market research clearly indicated, immediately after the festive period was a great time to advertise. It appeared to me that many people had got over the stress and expense of preparing for Christmas and they needed something to look forward to, especially in the UK when the long dark nights had closed in and the cold, depressing weather was upon them. Then, as if by magic, the adverts from major travel companies would appear on their TV screens showing beautiful places, with sun drenched beaches and that seemed enough to get their spending senses going again. When those adverts appeared, there was always a very strong emphasis placed upon holidays in Florida. Everywhere I seemed to look, all that I could see and hear was Florida.

Maybe, every cloud, and every cold dark UK winters cloud, does have a silver lining after all!

Although everyone may have their own methods and their own way of dealing with things, my systems, including the advertising strategy were intended to be simple but effective. Although I had very limited computer skills, I could do the essentials such as send e-mails with attachments, create files and basic spread sheets. My computerised records would be very basic to start with, however, I knew that they would develop as I progressed.

My systems were probably old fashioned in some respects. The reason for this was simply that I would create, work on and keep everything on computer to make things easy. However, I kept a paper based system as back up and whatever was on computer was printed off and kept in lever arch files. I copied absolutely everything, including cheques that I received from customers and all correspondence or office notes. I also recorded any significant dates, such as when I received payment from customers, when money was paid into the business bank account and precise details, including the time, of any conversations with customers. Why do that you may ask?

My answer was very simple, what happens if for whatever reason I lose all of my computer records due to some technical problem or what if the computer is stolen? My business would be well and truly in difficulties and I would have found it hard to recover from such a devastating blow. I know that many people will say, just back everything up on disc, well I did, but I took no chances and paper records were also kept. The other reason was just in case a customer made any complaint at all I would have an original record of everything as way of a safeguard. Each to their own I suppose!

I had most other administrative items, such as letter heads, draft pro-forma letters (which were adapted to meet individual requirements and which would save time on each enquiry), together with my filing system, well in hand and all that I had to do was bring it all together and make it specific and personal to my new property and my customers.

All of my correspondence was sent by first class post and all of my stationery was of good quality. That was particularly important to create the right professional image as soon as the customer received and opened the package. It would look right and feel right and I saw that issue as being one of great importance to my corporate image. It was all about the high quality of service, attention to detail and personal care of the customer. I also wanted the customer to have absolute confidence in me and my business and that way, they would be happy and spread the good word.

As part of my administrative system, I kept desk diaries for every year and this was an essential tool in keeping track of what was going on. I always bought diaries which had one full page for every day of the year as this provided sufficient space to make all of the necessary entries and as the business grew, many of those days had multiple entries as there were more and more customers booking their holidays or purchasing products from me. That system allowed me to see very clearly, on a day to day basis, exactly what was required and allowed me to prepare well in advance so that nothing was missed.

The whole process in relation to my desk diaries was meticulous, with built in safe guards to ensure that it was not possible for me to miss anything or make any mistakes. The entries in the diaries would be made immediately despite whatever else might be going on at the time, and I would re-check those entries against significant dates as I processed each and every booking. I also checked the diaries on a daily basis, once again, as a safeguard. It only took a minute and that in fact was the first job of the day, so nothing crept up on me and nothing caught me out unexpectedly.

Each time I confirmed a guest booking, the entries under specific relevant dates would include, for example:-

1. Name of the customer.
2. Customer unique reference number e.g. 1/08, 2/08 etc.
3. Date of arrival and specific holiday property address (this became critical as the business grew and I placed guests into holiday accommodation owned by other people.)
4. Any additional services i.e. vehicle hire, theme park or attraction tickets, telephone cards, swimming pool heating etc.
5. Date of departure from the property.
6. Ten weeks before their date of arrival at the holiday property, a preparation letter, which was basically a gentle reminder that their final balance payment would be due in two weeks time, would be sent to the client.
7. Eight weeks before date of arrival at the holiday property, the final balance payment from the customer would be due. Once received, the Guest Information Pack (Pack B) would be sent to the client.
8. Four weeks before date of arrival at the property, the final balance payment would be paid to the owner of the holiday

accommodation. (This related to guest bookings placed into many other holiday properties).

9. Two weeks after departing the property, return security deposit to customer.

People were paying a lot of money for a holiday and I could not afford to make any mistakes such as getting dates wrong or double booking property. The last thing that I wanted was, for example, to have one set of guests in a property and the day before they were due to leave, have another set of guests turn up at the door trying to gain access all because I had made a mistake with the availability dates. You may think that it would never happen, but I know that it did to some other property owners, as they firstly had not paid enough attention to what they were doing, secondly, their systems were not fail safe, and thirdly they would contact other property owners in a state of panic trying to sort out the mess.

Not the best start to the holiday for the guests and what must they have thought of the villa owner? In addition, if the owner did not do something very special indeed to recover the situation, you could probably write those people off as future business as they would be very reluctant to re-book ever again!

Invariably, property owners would not take a one or two night booking unless they made sure that the cleaning costs of such a short stay were also being paid by the panicking villa owner. Whether it was a one night booking or a 21 night booking, whenever guests rented the property, it had to be cleaned after they left and bed linen etc. had to be washed and changed. It all cost money and normally, it was the property owner who had made the mistake who lost out and had to fork out extra cash to cover the problem. The moral of the story being have sound, robust systems in place to prevent it from occurring in the first place and complete all of your administrative tasks immediately after you receive each enquiry or have any contact with a customer. Do not delay!

A diary system, whether created and updated on computer or recorded in paper form, is absolutely essential to ensure that your business flows and to prevent mistakes being made. The other essential part of this particular system is to ensure that you always have an up to date calendar at hand of your available dates. The reason being is so that when you receive an enquiry, whether by telephone, e-mail or in person, you can give the client an answer straight away. You know exactly what you need to do, and by that I mean, if you can not accommodate the enquiry because you have other guests in your home at that time, you can still provide a service to the customer and you can still generate income from them in such situations.

I really did not like the thought of saying no to someone who was potentially going to give me money and to say to them "Sorry I'm full" was doing exactly that. That was simply not providing a service and it was lost revenue and a lost opportunity for me. I sat and thought this through and I soon realised that due to the amount of free advertising that I had immediately secured, I had managed to fill just about everyday in that year, the following year and even some weeks into the third year of owning my property with confirmed bookings. I classed a booking as confirmed when I had actually received the returned signed booking form along with the deposit payment from the customer and, if the deposit payment had been made by cheque, when the cheque had cleared in my bank account. I was still receiving multiple enquiries from potential guests on a daily basis and it was clear to me that I had some good opportunities to seize upon.

In relation to confirmed bookings, always be aware of the person who says to you that they want to rent your property and give specific dates, yet no payment appears from them. If you do not receive their payment, give them a set period of time to get it to you, and I suggest days and not weeks, otherwise you may create a problem for yourself. That problem manifests itself in the following way. You may find that you turn away other potential guests who really want to rent the same period of time in your holiday home, and when it comes to the crunch, the person who said that they wanted to book your property in the first place lets you down and completely changes their mind. You are then left high and dry with empty spaces in your calendar of available dates and lost revenue. First come, first served is a sound way of securing income, especially in the early days of property ownership when you invariably need the money.

As your business grows and as you become more confident, you then realise that there are other methods of ensuring that you do not disappoint any customer and you could actually place them in other suitable accommodation.

When I looked at this problem I immediately realised that an opportunity existed to work with and assist other property owners, especially those who were not doing as well as me in relation to confirmed bookings. My idea was a basic and very simple one. It revolved around a Customer Referral System (CRS), which would enhance the opportunity for all involved in it to increase the number of confirmed bookings and in turn, boost their income and hopefully reduce their advertising costs by being more target specific. I was very much aware that there were numerous property owners that I knew who had good quality short term rental holiday accommodation in close proximity of one another yet they were working in isolation. They were spending a small fortune on narrow focussed and very limited advertising space in national newspapers and magazines, and it was apparent that it generally had a poor return for the costs involved. Many had their property advertised along side each other in the same small columns of newspapers. In effect they were battling it out against one another and it was clear to me that greater opportunities were out there and that all I had to do was harness and somehow control it.

As I have outlined, some advertising can be very expensive and if you have not thought things through and you do not have a clearly identified advertising strategy, with in-built monitoring systems to measure effectiveness, it could drain your resources and produce very little in terms of generating income.

That is when some property owners are in danger of falling into the cycle that I mentioned earlier where disillusionment and negativity sets in.

The CRS had to be firstly equal, fair and effective to all of those owners who wanted to become part of it. In addition, it was essential that everyone involved 'did their bit' to contribute to its, and ultimately, their own success. As the saying goes, you only get out of something what you put into it! That, and trust, were the very foundation on which it was to be built. I am not a naive person and have to say at this point that 'trust' did concern me and I find it a very interesting word indeed!

I spoke with a number of property owners and outlined my proposal and it was very well received. There had to be some basic rules of course and essentially this was to ensure that all owners still did their own advertising to prevent them from just sitting back and relying on others spending money to attract enquiries from which others who had spent little or nothing could benefit from. It was all about equal contribution and the way that it worked was, briefly, if an owner attracted an enquiry from a potential customer, but they could not accommodate them due to not having the required dates available, that owner would forward the details to the single point of contact who would possess up to date calendars of each owner who was part of the system. A check would be made to see which owner(s) had the availability and the contact details of the potential customer, and any additional helpful information would be forwarded to them to make contact with the customer.

The system had to be fair and the way that it worked out was if there were more than one owner who had the dates available, the owner who had contributed the most referrals into the system to help others, would get first bite of the cherry.

There were two things that concerned me about the CRS. Firstly, I wanted to keep it within my control as I could see the long term benefits and growth opportunities of such a system if it developed, but that was going to be problematic as I often worked long and unpredictable hours. Secondly, if I could not keep it within my control, who could I approach to operate the system and be that single point of contact?

After spending some time pondering the issues, I had no alternative but to reluctantly approach someone with some limited experience in this particular field to see if they would be willing to be that single point of contact. I had my reservations about that, but at that time, I had no alternative.

I knew that it would be a time consuming task and therefore the person who would operate the system needed to receive some kind of payment. That, in itself, threw up the issue of who would pay that person and how much would they receive?

The answer to the problem was that if an owner put a customer into the CRS and another owner managed to get a confirmed booking from it, then the owner who confirmed the booking would pay a set fee to the person who referred it in the first place and they would also pay a small set handling fee to the person operating the system. May sound a little complicated at first, however, what this did in effect was to create an incentive for owners to refer potential guests whom they could not accommodate into the system, as they would have an opportunity of receiving additional income for simply sending a fax, e-mail or even making a telephone call. That would ensure that the system would work, as without any referrals, the system would just wither on the vine.

This payment also assisted owners in covering their advertising costs by actually getting something back from what otherwise would have been a lost opportunity had they not been able to refer the customer to another owner. It also ensured that the person operating the system received payment for their time and work.

This system really encouraged some owners to contribute and they saw some good returns as a result. That, in turn, helped to provide them with a support mechanism which kept them motivated and enthusiastic about their venture and which created a network of contacts with people who were in a similar position to themselves.

Generally, it started off as a good and effective system and I received many calls on a daily basis from property owners who required information or asked for guidance about many wide and varied issues, but particularly in relation to marketing and advertising.

There was a little more to the system than I have outlined and although I had sat down and thought things through about the whole process, it had to work on a trust basis, with maximum contribution by each and every member.

Some of the most important things in relation to ensuring the effective operation of the CRS surrounded issues such as availability calendars of individual owners, ensuring that the correct contact details and information was initially obtained from potential customers, ensuring immediate contact with customers, and prompt payment of referral fees to other members.

I certainly did not have time to chase up owners who did not keep their availability calendars up to date and it was neither my responsibility, nor the person who was operating the system, to do that. It was made clear from the start that the responsibility sat fairly and squarely on the shoulders of the individual owners to keep the system updated and if they did not and lost out, or if it caused the system operator to believe that an owner had availability when in fact they had not and just repeatedly failed to contact the system operator and update them, then it was down to them if they did not receive any further referrals.

It was apparent that when some owners spoke with potential customers, they did not always ask sufficient questions or obtain even basic contact details which were crucial in assisting to convert the call from an initial enquiry into a confirmed booking and ultimately into cash.

Sometimes they had not even obtained the basics such as the full name of the customer or even on occasions a telephone number, and just how are you expected to do something with that? I have spent many hours trying to trace people through telephone books or via companies when supplied with extremely limited information by contributors. A frustrating task indeed!

To prevent this from happening, I devised a basic form which could be completed in just a few seconds when owners were speaking with customers and it ensured that sufficient information would be obtained to make the whole process workable and less time consuming.

If you think of the essentials such as full name, postal and e-mail address, daytime and evening landline telephone number, mobile telephone number, dates of travel including specific number of nights required in private holiday accommodation, total number of people in the party – including a breakdown of the number of adults and children (required for sleeping / bedroom arrangements), preferred location and type of property i.e. three or four bedroom detached property with swimming pool, Jacuzzi spa, games room etc. any additional information such as flights, vehicle hire, theme park or attraction tickets required?

You can see from that how much easier it is when you have the information at hand and you are more prepared when you actually speak with any potential customer.

Once you receive an enquiry, it is essential that you make contact with that person at the earliest opportunity. If you don't, there is a very strong likelihood that they will go to someone else and you will have lost out. If they are unavailable or you can't speak with them for whatever reason, leave a message or try and get the information to them in some other way, as that will let them know that you have tried to contact them straight away, you are there to help and that you are reliable. That was a particular concern with some owners in the CRS and this could have effected the professional reputation that was so important to me and revenue could have been lost.

As a way of building trust and confidence in the system, I encouraged property owners to keep a copy of the details of people whom they had referred into the system as that way, everyone would know that the customer could be contacted at any time to see how far things had progressed and if they had actually booked with another owner. It sent out the message from the start that things had to be done correctly, otherwise property owners would be at risk of forfeiting their membership.

All that I will say about the CRS is that it had great potential and really did assist some owners. However, after devising the system, contacting many owners and getting the concept up and running, I became disillusioned with its operational effectiveness.

I did not have the capacity at that time to manage the system personally and was reliant upon others to do so. I became concerned about certain aspects of it and as a result I tactfully distanced myself from the whole process. Overall, I had my good reputation and professional image to think about, and that was something that I would not sacrifice on any account.

I often take the view that sometimes things happen in life for a reason, only at the time, the reason may not always be that clear. As a result of my experience of the Customer Referral System, I later went on to really develop a whole knew business concept which grew into something which I could never have imagined. The list of services to customers increased, and the amount of turnover generated by the business was incredible. The only thing that determined how big it would grow was the amount of time that I could devote to the business due to my daytime job.

As part of my original administrative set up, I was aware that there were other essential elements which I needed to consider, such as a web site for my property, an e-mail address so that contact with people would be made easier, and a business telephone and fax facility.

I had already made arrangements to have a web site constructed and as soon as I returned home, the selected images that I had taken were put onto my web site and all of the information was then uploaded onto the World Wide Web. That, I have to say, was probably the best tool that I had in my business armoury!

The web site was a great way of making sales. If anyone contacted me by telephone and they were on-line, I could give them the web site address and they could view it straight away. That also meant that I could actually talk them through it and put my sales pitch to good use. The vast majority of my sales were eventually captured that way and it was probably the best way of striking when the iron was hot!

My web site was very attractive on the eye. It was colourful, it looked warm and welcoming, it was very easy to navigate and extremely user friendly. My contact details were clear and provided both landline and mobile telephone numbers, my full business postal address and my e-mail address. I had also included an e-mail link, which meant that if the customer preferred, they could just contact me direct from the site and start the whole process rolling.

That's when your well thought out images really do come into there own!

I wanted customers to know about the business and what professional services I could offer. I encouraged them to ask questions of me and how the business worked and I have no doubt at all that as a result, I secured many more confirmed bookings.

As a side issue and one which I believe to be very important in relation to inspiring business confidence in customers, when you choose the e-mail address that you will be using to correspond with customers, please spend just a little time thinking about the professional image that you are trying to portray. The reason that I say that is because, over the years, I have seen some completely outrageous and almost offensive e-mail addresses being used to attract and correspond with customers and to be honest about it, if I was a potential customer, after just seeing the e-mail address, I would have walked away. For obvious reasons, I am not going to outline the ones that I have seen, but it is suffice to say, don't choose an e-mail address which looks unprofessional and portrays the wrong impression.

I had decided to have a separate telephone line installed in my office which would be dedicated as the business telephone and fax number. In reality, when that telephone rang, everything that I was doing stopped immediately and it was answered without any delay. That was my money line!

Taking into consideration that I have never been a salesperson in my life, I had to really think about what I would say to customers when I spoke with them. I did not want to go into anything cold and therefore I prepared what I would need to say and what I believed to be the best way of saying it. I actually rehearsed what I would say and how I would say it. When I spoke with a customer, part of my sales technique was that I was always warm, friendly, professional and confident in the products and services that I had to offer. I knew my product and as I got more and more confident when speaking with customers and the confirmed bookings started to materialise, I realised what it was that was actually clinching that deal!

Two things had stood out amongst everything else and many of my customers were telling me what had made them book with me as opposed to the large number of other holiday home owners that they had spoken with. It had to be right as everyone was saying the same thing and they did not know one another. The two things that jumped out above everything else was my sheer enthusiasm and passion about holidays in Florida and the high level of service that I could offer when I spoke with customers. I thoroughly enjoyed speaking with them and I knew that I used to get excited about every aspect of Florida and that was clearly coming across during my many conversations. It actually got the customers excited and when they saw the web site, listened to what I was saying and the professional approach that I always took, it really got them on the hook and the confirmed bookings came in thick and fast. I have to say that I developed a real knack for converting enquiries into confirmed bookings and, in turn, generating income. No wonder I got excited when I spoke with every customer, I was giving them a really good personal service and they were giving me lots of money in return! That to me, was the perfect approach to business.

I have to say that I was always honest and open and answered any questions that the customer may have had. I was never evasive and if I couldn't answer a particular question straight away, I would always find the answer to that question and ring the customer back as soon as possible. That in itself provided me with two things. Firstly, the opportunity to speak with the customer again and secondly, it clearly displayed that I was giving them my personal and undivided attention to meet their needs or requirements and I was making them feel special.

I am a firm believer in the fact that if you want someone to buy something from you, make them feel very special indeed, because that is exactly what they are.

One thing that I had learned very early on whilst I was doing my research was that even when some holiday property owners were advertising their homes for rental purposes, they appeared to be very unreliable. I lost count of the number of telephone messages that I left or e-mails that I sent where I did not even get the courtesy of a reply. To this day I am still not sure why that happened, maybe they just could not be bothered, maybe they had fallen into the downward spiral as I described earlier and they had become disillusioned or maybe they did not need the money from rentals, but if that was the case why were they spending money on advertising in the first place?

As a result of that experience, I knew from the very start that I had to be contactable all of the time and make sure that if I could not be contactable due to my daytime commitments, that my telephone was diverted to someone who could speak with the callers. I did not want to be in a position or take the risk of a customer trying to contact me on the telephone and if I was not there to take the call, to allow them to slip away and go to another property owner. Once again, that would be a lost opportunity and loss of potential revenue. As a result, I made immediate arrangements to prevent that from happening and to ensure that I had something in place to cover the times when, for whatever reason, I was not in a position to divert my business landline and take the calls on my mobile telephone, that someone else could take the calls on my behalf.

It's strange what you pick up from speaking with people and it may be very easy to make your mind up or even judge someone after just speaking with them for a short period of time on a telephone. The reason why I say this is because of my experience of speaking with many property owners, especially in my early days when carrying out my research.

I soon became aware of a number of things such as how the owner answered the telephone, what they said, how they said it, the tone of their voice and, of all things, background noise and other distractions.

Baring in mind, as I was looking for accommodation to stay in for a week out there so that I could do business, I was speaking with some owners as a potential customer, however, you would think that on occasion I had misdialled and telephoned the undertakers instead!

Talk about poor communication skills and lack of enthusiasm, some were so dour that it threw me and I almost became stuck for words myself. It was like pulling teeth trying to get information out of some of them and at times, as a result of their response to me, I felt that I had actually inconvenienced some owners by ringing them. Maybe it was a lack of confidence on their part, however as a potential customer that would have really turned me away from doing any business at all with owners like that. Whatever happened to warm, friendly and welcoming?

I can not stress enough that telephone manner is so incredibly important when speaking with customers. Know your product, be organised and have information at hand, such as a copy of your brochure to refer to and maps of the area to assist the customer in visualising where they would be staying on holiday in relation to the location of the airport, any local beaches and any major tourist attractions.

Be confident in your ability, your product, your sales pitch, your services to customers and in yourself. If you are confident, it washes off onto the customers and they become confident in you and what you have to offer. It is all about reassuring the customer that their needs will be catered for and you can deliver the service that you say you can. You have to work at it to win the trust and confidence of each and every customer. If you take your time you'll win their confidence and you will reap the rewards.

The issue of background noise and distractions hit me like a ton of bricks. There I was, in the eyes of the property owner, a potential customer looking to find private rental accommodation. I was about to give them a large amount of my money and in doing so I was looking for that trust and confidence factor in return, which would have convinced me to do so. However, all that I, the customer could hear in the background on occasions were screaming kids, the whirling of a washing machine or tumble dryer and even the sound of a toilet being flushed! Just who the hell was I speaking with?

It really put me off and on one or two occasions, owners interrupted me and said "Can you hang on a second" and then I would hear them bellow at the top of their voices at the kids to shut up, be quiet and get out. I know that kids being kids are noisy, but when you are trying to run a business, you really need to be aware of your surroundings and the impression that you are creating for the customer otherwise they will just walk away. Apart from that, the bellowing shrieks did my eardrums no favours whatsoever!

Whenever a customer contacts you, always ask them where they saw your advert or where they obtained your contact details. As I mentioned earlier, advertising can be very expensive and you need to have a system in place to identify where your best source of advertising comes from. As part of that process, you will also be able to monitor all of your other sources of advertising, how much it is costing and what is the actual return in terms of confirmed bookings.

If you do not ask each and every customer the question, you will have little or no idea as to what is effective and you could end up throwing away good money after bad. If that happens and you get little in the way of generating income, then it may become a downward spiral. Avoid that at all costs by asking the simple question, where did you see my advert?

I always paid particular attention to that issue and every week I would assess and reassess my advertising strategy. That way, you are constantly on top of it and you can change course if it is clear that a certain advert is not working.

If you find a golden thread where your advertising return is significantly higher in terms of confirmed bookings, guard that source with everything that you have. Do not tell anyone else as the next thing that you know there will be dozens of property owners fighting to get a cut of the action. Keep it to yourself and do not kill the golden goose!

As a result of taking and retaining the details of each person that contacts you, over a period of time you will find that you have built up quite a considerable data base of clients. Taking into account and complying with the requirements of the Data Protection Act in the UK, this is a very useful tool and can be an integral part of your advertising strategy. Those very people have taken the time to contact you, and whether they booked with you or not, they have expressed an interest in the area where your property is located and they are the right people to target in the future. An effective way of staying in touch with them all is by way of a monthly or bi-monthly newsletter. That can be done either via the post or, if you have their e-mail addresses, electronically.

It is obviously up to you what you include in such a letter, however, it has to be informative, hold their interest, tell them what services you have available, any special offers or discounts and items of special interest which may attract them to your holiday home. Items of special interest could, for example, relate to major tourist attractions in the area, local festivals, activities, arts, crafts, beaches, water sports, wildlife, retail and bargain type outlets, fashion, local food and produce and above all, the climate compared to that of the UK at various times of the year. Anything exciting or different about the area that may entice the customer to contact you is worthy of inclusion as long as you get your personal message across.

A good source of research for such materials is obviously the internet where you will probably find enough up to date information to keep your newsletter fresh and attractive. You can now see a more scientific picture building as you target more and more people who have a clear interest in the location of your property.

When you start to receive enquiries from customers it is a strangely exciting time. You will have probably heard on many occasions the words "Please hold, your message is important to us" or something very similar, when you have tried to get through to some companies but the lines are always engaged. Well, from day one, I always took the view that anyone of those calls from potential customers could put money into my pocket and therefore each one was extremely important to me and I really meant that!

I had thought long and hard about what prices I would charge customers for renting my home and it was a difficult one to work out at first. It was essential that I covered all of my costs and I would not, and could not, subsidise other people's holidays. I also had to strike a balance where I was competitive whilst trying to make a profit as well.

I did an immense amount of research into price structures and I found that after all of that time and work, I could not for the life of me work out how so many owners could offer so many different prices for what was a very similar product. I put properties into categories such as the number of bedrooms and bathrooms, locations, views, developments, new property, old property, extras such as Jacuzzi spa's, games rooms, communal and recreational facilities such as tennis courts, play areas etc. etc., and I could not find any sure formula at all.

My research concluded three things, and those were prices which were middle of the road, prices that were ridiculously low and prices which, in my view, were so over the top that the only way of describing them would be with the words obscenely greedy.

That in itself reassured me to some extent as I believed that owners who were looking to charge such incredibly high prices would price themselves out of the market, which in turn might drive customers toward me. My view in relation to high pricing, and one which was formed over a number of years, was that there were generally two types of owner that charged such high prices. The first were those people who were new to the game and either thought that they could actually command the income they received based upon an inflexible 'take it or leave it' customer pricing policy. Secondly, those owners who thought that they would try it out and see if they could get top dollar out of customers each and every time.

Invariably in relation to both types of owner, the customer would leave it and give them a very wide berth indeed. Why should they spend more money than necessary when there were so many properties on the market to choose from?

That takes me to property being advertised for short term rental at ridiculously low prices. There may have been many reasons why owners did this, and I had several thoughts about it. Maybe they just did not know the market, maybe the price reflected the standard or location of their property or were they in such a desperate financial state that they would do just about anything to get a few customers in through the front door and rent their home?

Customers need to know exactly how much it will cost them for a holiday and the issue of pricing will always come up in any conversation or communication. When the internet came along, it brought with it so many opportunities, that it changed our world forever. One such opportunity would be extremely advantageous for consumers and this allowed them to sit in the comfort of their own homes and purchase virtually anything and everything that they needed on-line. That would also include holidays and arguably, it has changed the whole way that many tourists prepare their travel plans. The days when we would have had little choice but to go to high street travel agents to get what we wanted are long gone and the internet has allowed us to buy all or any part of a holiday at the click of a mouse and the touch of a button on a keyboard.

The result of that has meant consumers can very easily browse the vast number of holiday homes located all over the world that are advertised and available to rent. It also means that, as opposed to having to buy a package holiday direct from travel agents, consumers can arrange each and every part of their holiday separately if they so require. It is so easy to arrange to rent a holiday home from an owner, and then book flights on line with one company and vehicle hire with another and so on. That has completely opened up the market and competition has arguably never been so great. All in all, very good news for consumers, however that places more demands on property owners who need to be more creative and imaginative when advertising their property in order to stave off any competition and secure their rental income.

I believe that this is one of the main reasons why you see some properties being advertised at ridiculously low prices as some owners battle it out with each other in some kind of price war. My personal view is that the only loser there is the actual property owners as they are cutting prices so far to the bone that they can barely cover the monthly expenditure, if not at all in some cases. I have also known low prices to have an adverse effect on customer confidence in that they have seen the property advertised at such a low price they become very suspicious indeed and question the standard of what they could be spending their money on. The last thing that any customer wants is to arrive at the rental home to find that it is run down and in a generally poorly maintained condition. They would have no choice but to stay there for the duration of their holiday or spend more time and money looking for alternative accommodation and then have to fight it out with the property owner to recover any costs or compensation when they return home.

The approach that I took in relation to identifying an appropriate price structure was initially based upon my monthly expenditure and what income that I had to generate just to break even. With that figure in mind, I then looked at the different holiday seasons in any one year and, very simplistically, broke it down to high, medium and low categories.

The high season would obviously be what it said, when demand was at its peak, such as the Easter period, summer school and half term holidays, Christmas and the New Year festive period.

The low season basically included the first three months of January, February and March, and excluded any school or public holidays.

The medium season would be any other time of the year.

Now that I had my monthly target figure and my seasons identified I looked very closely at profit margin and based that upon two different price structures. Firstly I would have a general pricing structure for the 'unknown customer' and secondly, I had my 'mates rates' which was the discounted price for anyone that I knew, such as friends, family, work colleagues and for all of those people who contacted me as a result of me being allowed to advertise free of charge in some of the large organisations that I mentioned earlier.

Although I had two different structures, I still included the essential element of profit. Some people may raise an eyebrow when I mention taking money from family members who want to take a holiday and stay in your rental home. It is an individual choice, but remember, you are running a business and one which will cost you money every month and it is not a charity. My parents did of course stay in my property free of charge, which was clearly a pleasure for me to do and was not a problem. However, for extended family members it may be a different case altogether and you may find that many friends and some family members will expect or even assume that they will be able to stay in your property either free of charge or at an outrageously low price. My view is that they should think again!

I made the very conscious decision that my prices would include a fairly healthy profit margin, but I also made the decision that it may be better to actually charge a little less and secure more confirmed bookings as opposed to taking the risk of charging as much as possible and losing potential customers, pricing myself out of the market and generating much less income. The balance had to be right and I knew that if I was going to do that, I would need to identify a way of making up that reduction. As a result of my research, I knew that I had some very good ideas for generating income by offering additional services and that would be a window of opportunity to really boost my overall turnover and increase profit margins.

When it came to the crunch, I was satisfied that I had my price structures in place, however, I was also flexible in my approach. That flexibility, as mentioned above, came in the form of identifying opportunities when it may be better to charge a little less to attract a smaller family or group of people to rent my home as opposed to going for maximum possible income, but have a much larger party staying in my property. My rationale behind that decision was, for example, if there were a party of only four people staying in the property, there will be less general wear and tear on the home and the utility bills will be much less than when, for example, a party of ten stay in the home. I would rather have smaller numbers of people in my home at any one time as opposed to a full house when everything would get absolutely hammered!

This was also a very useful approach indeed when speaking with customers and this went on to form a major part of my sales technique. Everyone loves a bargain or discount and if they can get a reduction in price then generally people always feel a little better about the whole thing.

Over the years, I have lost count of the number of people who have come to me for information, assistance or guidance when they were thinking about purchasing property abroad for short term rental purposes

I spent hours with them and went into every detail that I could to help them make informed decisions. There were obviously things that I had done initially which, if I were starting out again, I may do differently now and I was also quite happy to tell them about my research, approach to business, my personal experiences and any problems that I had encountered along the way.

Taking into account that many of those people had no experience at all about this type of business and all that they really had was their dream of owning property in a sunny foreign climate, the attitude of some never ceased to amaze me.

I have always taken the view that if I don't know the answer to something I will ask someone who does know or I research the issue until I come up with the right answer. What I found time and time again was that some of the people that came to me for information would try and suck my brains dry and get as much as they could out of me, then if they actually purchased a home abroad, within a short space of time they would try and tell me what to do and how I should operate my business.

I am of course fully aware that people can do their own thing and whatever they do is their own personal choice, however, the arrogance of some simply astounded me. To enter into a new venture and especially one such as this and then almost cut their own throats by offending people whom could actually help them was almost beyond belief.

Many would be adamant that they were right about so many issues, especially, that of what price they would charge customers. Many said that they would be inflexible with pricing, that they had fixed prices in place and that they would stick it out to get top dollar. Taking into consideration what I said earlier about my predictions, which in my opinion, generally occur in the first 12 – 36 months after taking possession of their property, unless these new property owners could afford to own a property abroad without having to rely on rental income to pay the monthly bills, they would have to change their attitude and their approach to business or suffer the consequences. One thing that I did see was that the attitude of such people created another business opportunity for me. All that I would have to do is wait, and just maybe, when they found themselves in a position when they realised that they could not attract sufficient paying guests to cover their operating costs, they would then listen to someone who knew what they were doing and indeed someone who could actually capture sufficient paying customers to help them, which in turn, would generate even more income for me!

One of the most significant things that came from my approach and my overall sales technique was the issue of repeat customers. I took real pride in the quality of service that I offered and the result was that my customers had great holidays, they received discounts whenever possible, they spread the word to lots of other people and they, along with others with whom they had told, came back to me year after year. This made things much easier to deal with and this actually assisted me to keep costs down in relation to advertising. I also incorporated many other things into my sales technique and overall package, such as discounts on a number of other services.

In relation to personal recommendation, as I have already said, as far as I am concerned there is nothing better than word of mouth!

The business that I generated grew rapidly and the golden thread that ran through my success in attracting paying guests to rental homes across the State of Florida was directly linked to word of mouth recommendation. I had so many people who contacted me and firstly said that I did not know them, however they new me through their friends, family members or work colleagues who had booked their holidays with me, and the feedback I have to say was very complimentary indeed.

That was exactly what I was looking for from the very first day of launching my business.

As my business developed I soon realised that there were certain times of the year which, if it were possible, I could sell over and over again. A perfect example of this is the Easter, summer and half term school holidays and the Christmas period, which are always in great demand. You will probably find that those dates will fill up your calendar of availability first, however, be aware of the fact that some people may only want to book one week in your home. If that occurs, before you accept the booking, take a closer look at the dates, as you may find that if you accept that one week booking, you may have to forfeit bookings either side of those dates and it will have prevented you from possibly placing more and longer bookings into your property.

You may decide to keep a one week booking rather than disappoint a customer, however, if you decide against it, you may want to contact another property owner and offer it to them as it might just fill up any odd gaps in their calendar.

The final thing that I would say in relation to pricing is do not let greed overcome your judgement. Be flexible, take a little less on some of the smaller party bookings if you can. As they say, 'Less is more'!

The whole aspect of receiving money from customers is, for me, very exciting and extremely rewarding indeed. When the 'posty' arrives at your door and you see the envelopes fall onto the mat, that is when it makes everything that you have done very worthwhile indeed.

In only a very short space of time, I was receiving envelopes containing cheques on a daily basis and my business bank account soon started to swell. The whole aspect of method of payment from customers is one which would appear to be easy, yet there are a number of difficulties surrounding the issue. As we now live in a world of the internet and the credit card, just about every customer will want to pay you with some kind of credit or debit card. I initially thought that it would not be a problem and it would be a simple task of basically going to a bank or other supplier, filling in the forms, showing that I was a safe risk and I would be able to get a facility to take payment in that form. After all, everywhere that I went I would see businesses of all shapes and sizes taking payment from customers who wanted to pay with plastic. Nothing could be further from the truth!

'Not a chance' was the message from the high street banks and the reason that they gave for refusing such a facility was not me as a person, as I had a very good credit rating indeed. It was down to the fact that all they could see was that I was in the travel industry and I was not ABTA or ATOL bonded. Without such a bond it was an absolute non-starter.

The whole issue of ABTA and ATOL bonds is a very complicated one indeed and the process is too long winded to describe at this point. It is suffice to say that, as a starting point, you have to walk before you can run and you need to build up your business, have the necessary funds and supporting accountancy documentation behind you to secure a bond. As they say, for further information, visit their web site and see for yourself the whole application process and associated requirements.

The problem in relation to method of payment boils down to one of two things. Basically, unless you can use or secure some other alternative arrangement to take payment on credit or debit cards, you can only take payment in the form of cheques or cash.

That in itself can cause so much concern as when a customer wants to pay by plastic card and you tell them that you can not take payment in that form, there is invariably a lack of confidence that pervades and concerns are raised by the customer. The general concerns revolve around consumer protection should anything go wrong. That is when you really need to reassure the customer that you are professional in every aspect of your business and that nothing will go wrong. Over the years, I was only able to do that due to the care and attention I paid to detail from the very first day in business. I had very few concerns raised by customers with whom I had supplied various services. Those that did raise an issue were given guidance and support from myself. The things that were raised were often out of my control and had absolutely nothing to do with the services that I had either offered or supplied, or with my business in general. If any issue, concern or complaint was raised by a customer and though totally unrelated to my business, I would still go out of my way to assist them in any way that I could. An obvious example of this being flight delays. Once again, I wanted to provide a very good quality of service and one which they, the customer, would always remember.

Everything that I did was with the intention of getting customers to come back to me in the future and spread the word to others in the mean time and that approach certainly worked and was very successful indeed.

You will recall that, at the start of my business venture, I decided to keep my personal finances and my business finances completely separate and that was, what I believe to be, a very wise decision indeed. I was aware of so many people who only had one bank account and everything went through that, whether it was business or personal. Those people soon got into quite a mess, and caused themselves problems, especially in relation to business income and expenditure, general accountancy records and end of year tax issues.

I had no doubt that having completely separate business and personal bank accounts and small business bankers to assist me both in the UK and, in my case Florida, was clearly the right thing to do and made things so much easier to manage and I never experienced any problems at all.

The whole issue of banking and record keeping to me is an essential element of any business and I can not emphasise enough the importance of having good systems in place from the very start. Find a system that is straight forward, uncomplicated and one which suits you and meets all of your requirements.

Keep accurate records in relation to both income and expenditure, and make sure that you gather receipts for any expenditure that relates to your business. In relation to receipts, you will find that they will mount up very quickly, and once again, I can not stress the importance of recording them onto your system straight away and then filing them for future reference. If you leave them for any length of time it becomes an unwieldy task of sorting them out and it's much easier and less time consuming if you do the job straight away as opposed to at the end of the month, or longer as the case may be. It will also show that you are organised and will therefore free up your time to prioritise other important tasks such as advertising and generating even more income.

When I first realised my dream and purchased my property in Florida, you may recall that I sat in a rocking chair in the sunshine, beside the lake in the town of Celebration, drinking fresh coffee from Barnies coffee shop and watched the turtles and fish swimming right up to me. As I sat there I was thinking about the future and how I could make money. It soon became very clear that I could generate quite a considerable sum of money even before the property was built and ready for the first guests to walk through the door.

This particular idea revolved around the issue of advertising and getting as many confirmed bookings as soon as I possibly could and that would be my main thrust from the moment that I returned home.

As I have outlined, I only considered a booking as confirmed when I had received either a deposit payment or full balance payment from a customer. That would mean if I could advertise and generate as many confirmed bookings as I could in the twelve months before the property was constructed and I took possession of it, I would receive a payment of £100.00 per week booked as way of deposit from customers. I knew that most customers would book at least two weeks for a holiday and, as it turned out, I was very pleased indeed with the number of three week bookings that I received. That would really boost my level of working capital, underpin my overall financial situation and provide an even stronger foundation to build upon. The only problem that I envisaged was trying to identify a completion date when I would actually take possession of the keys to the property.

I spoke with my realtor on a regular basis and it became clear that the development where I had purchased my property was now well on its way to being sold out and that the developers were working flat out to get properties completed on schedule.

I was given a target date for completion, and I added a few weeks to that date just in case of any slippage in the work schedule. That was my built in comfort zone just in case of any unexpected problems and I allowed something like six weeks after the target date before I would take in the first paying guests.

I had the target date for completion from the developers which greatly assisted my planning and they were very confident in meeting that date. Six weeks was still a good chunk of time as way of contingency and that would also allow me to travel out to Florida for the closing process, inspect the property for myself, make sure that everything was in place and make any additional purchases or final touches that may be necessary.

I have to say that I worked flat out when I returned home to generate those confirmed bookings and I was soon well on my way to filling up my available dates. One of the surprising things for me was how far in advance some customers wanted to book their holidays. I had to produce availability calendars for the following three years after the date of completion as I had some customers who were looking that far in advance. A vast majority of course wanted to confirm their bookings which predominantly fell during the period within eighteen months after the completion date.

I also found that time after time I would receive enquiries from customers who wanted to rent my property for the same dates that I had reserved for myself. I also found that I immediately gave up my dates to ensure that I secured customer bookings and generated more income which was crucial in the early days of my business. As time went by and my business grew, I found that I could afford to reserve dates for myself as firstly, if I did not, I would never have had the pleasure of staying in my own holiday home and secondly, I had developed and grown the business infrastructure to provide alternative accommodation for customers whereby I would still generate income by doing so. Basically, the customer came first and my planning and development ensured that I was in a win-win situation whereby the customer always got what they required and I made money out of it.

By the time the date came around for the closing process to take place, I had banked thousands of pounds in deposit payments and my decision to advertise at the earliest possible opportunity had really paid off.

It is worth mentioning at this juncture the issue of the closing process and the associated experiences that many new owners endure when they travel out to take possession of the keys to their property for the first time.

I have seen many new property owners go through a very frustrating and often stressful time, which has produced a wide and varied range of emotions when the time comes to take possession of their new home. Once again, I have lost count of the number of new owners with whom I have spoken over the years who were given a completion date to work too and they have booked and paid for flights, vehicle hire and accommodation to stay in before they get their hands on the keys and then, for whatever reason, the closing process is delayed or the property has not been completed on time. That is a certain recipe for high blood pressure and not a very nice position to be in, especially when you travel out, see your new home and have to return home without the process being completed.

I was very fortunate as I was in regular contact with my realtor and the developer involved and I had weekly progress reports. In addition, as I had regularly discussed progress, especially as we neared the completion date, it was also clear that it was in the best interest of the developers to complete on time as it not only effected my agreement with them, but it also effected their general development plans.

When I had originally researched that particular development prior to purchase, I saw that this was the first of two new major developments by the same construction company that would make up that particular short term rental area. I was told by the company realtor that they were desperate to complete the first development so that it portrayed the right image for passers by and become even more attractive for potential property buyers, which would in turn really kick start the sale of property on the second development once that site was opened up. It would also of course ensure that the developer made an incredible amount of money during the whole process.

The end result for me was fairly straight forward. As a result of the regular contact, especially on the build up to the target date, this ensured that my date and actual time of closing was confirmed and I even knew that it would take place in one of the private rooms at a specified show home on the development. I was able to make all of my final preparations, including sending out the final 10% of my deposit, and arrange my flights and vehicle hire. As I would be arriving the day before, I also arranged accommodation for the night.

As it turned out, my date of closing was in fact delayed by one day and that was due to the realtor being ill. As I was there for ten nights, this did not really cause me a great problem and I was still able to gain access to my new home and carry out a 'pre-inspection inspection'!

That delay was actually very useful as it gave me time alone to carry out a very detailed examination indeed. I went over everything, and I mean everything. Not a wall, drawer, cupboard, appliance or piece of furniture was missed and that included going over everything in the furniture package, down to making sure that the right amount of bedding, knives, forks, cups and plates were there. It was more like a finger tip search than an inspection. My inspection did identify a number of minor faults, but nothing serious. Examples of those faults included a hole near a waste pipe outlet under the kitchen sink which needed to be filled and decorated, one or two walls had scuff marks which would be redecorated and a table would be exchanged as it had a scratch on the top. Externally, there were two or three pieces of plaster work that needed some attention and a crack in part of the driveway which would be relayed and made good. Overall, I was very pleased with the quality of the build and I must add that the female site supervisor whom I mentioned much earlier had the relevant tradesmen lined up the following morning to make good the faults.

In a nutshell, make sure that your closing / completion date is confirmed before you book your flight and travel out, otherwise you could return home without the keys to your new property, only to have to do it all again when the property is ready.

Don't be put off by any realtor who says that it is not necessary for you to travel out to for closing. By travelling out, you can do your own inspection, as well as the one by your realtor, before you sign to take over the property. One final thought - be picky - it's your home, and satisfy yourself that everything is just as you wanted it and to the required standard!

Once you have the keys in your possession, you can really start to get your business moving. When I say business, that is exactly what I mean and that was the approach that I took from day one.

If you want to generate income, then take the view that owning and operating a holiday home abroad is a small business. If you treat it as exactly that, you will not go far wrong.

Make comparisons with what you may do for a living and the company or organisation that you may work for. Then think about how that company conducts business or how they operate on a day to day basis and how decisions are made.

If a large corporation or organisation does something or makes a decision and it does not work out or it is ineffective and costs them money, at the end of the day, they can just swallow up the cost and learn from those lessons. If you, as an individual, get things wrong and if you do not have strong financial support or infrastructure in place, it could be absolutely disastrous for you personally.

What I am saying is never be afraid to make decisions as there will be many to be made. However, you are doing this for real now, for yourself and not for some major company. The one lesson that I took from this over the years was very simple, and that was focus in on every little aspect of your plans, and think things through to the enth degree. As your business develops, revisit those plans and see if they are still effective. If they are not or they have been in place for some time and need refreshing, start planning again. There should be a constant rolling programme of identifying areas for development, planning, implementation and outcome assessment. It may sound complicated or even long winded, but it's not and once again, it worked for me and it seems to work for many other successful business people. If it is a way of putting money into your pocket, then it is worth the time and effort to explore the idea.

I found that I was constantly thinking of ways to put money into my pocket. It was a favourite pass time and I found that some ideas were very realistic and very successful indeed.

I also believed that I might have to give a little to make a lot more in the future!

My views were quite simple really and revolved around what I wanted to offer my customers. My promise to them included that any service that I offered or supplied would be first class, prompt and professional and would encompass 'the personal touch'. I wanted my customers to know that I had nothing but high standards, that I was totally reliable and that I offered great value for money. I also encouraged them to ask questions of me, my experience and how my business worked. I often found that transparency increased customer confidence, which in turn, generated income.

I always got a good feel for customers and what they were actually looking for in relation to their holiday. That was very important to me as this allowed me to develop my services to ensure that I could meet the customer's requirements and to offer customers just a little extra for nothing!

As I mentioned earlier, generally, I think it's fair to say that everyone wants good value for money and most people that I know are always looking for a good deal. With that in mind, I decided that wherever possible, I would give my customers something extra at no additional charge.

At first, the things that I would give were not large or expensive, but clearly showed that I had put the customer first and it was a nice, personal touch. The things that I would give them were for example, a free welcome food pack, which consisted of a few basic things such as bread, milk, eggs, bacon, orange juice and a bottle of wine. Alternatively I may have given them a free telephone card, which would allow them to telephone home at very cheap rates compared to them having to use a mobile at international rates or paying using a credit card.

If I was out there and was expecting guests to arrive, I would often leave a bottle of wine and wine glasses ready for them or even a few beers in the fridge, which would be nicely chilled for the guest's arrival.

These were little things which were inexpensive to supply and created a very good impression with my customers.

Just in relation to glass, I would also leave and had a good stock of plastic cups and plates etc. for use around the swimming pool, as you can only imagine what dangers could be caused if broken glass were on the pool deck area or worse still, in the swimming pool.

As time went on and the business developed, I actually gave customers small, but free, upgrades on rental vehicles or private villas. I also went out of my way to make sure that everything was just right, which in turn, would make the holiday stress free for my customers.

It was all about understanding the customer's needs, requirements and expectations. Some people may consider giving something for nothing was a foolish thing to do, however, remember what I said about giving a little to get an awful lot more? Well, that's exactly what happened and that's one of the reasons why I was so successful at attracting so many people who wanted to rent holiday accommodation.

Customers came back to me year after year, and very importantly, they spread the good word – great advertising at no extra cost!

As part of understanding the customers needs, I also supplied them with a very good 'Customer Information Pack', or my 'Pack B' as I named it. If you think back to what I said earlier, when I supplied initial information to potential customers, along with the booking form etc, that was what I named my 'Pack A'. When customers confirmed a booking with me I would need to send them a full client information pack, which they would receive eight weeks prior to their arrival date. The reason why I chose eight weeks prior to them arriving at the villa, was due to the fact that it coincided with their final balance payment to me. In effect, when I received their final payment, the customer would receive their very comprehensive information pack.

I have seen many documents from various holiday property owners that they send to people who have rented their property. I can only say that some are very good and, in my view, so many others are so poor and totally unprofessional that it beggars belief.

It is clear to see that some owners do actually take the time to provide good quality information to guests and provide it in an attractive, well thought out way. Unfortunately, some that I have seen can only be described, in my opinion, as absolute rubbish and totally unprofessional. The poor quality guest information documents that I have seen range from very badly photocopied black and white one page 'notes', to 'letters' which only contained an address of the holiday home and very brief and confusing directions. Some did not even include any contact details in relation to who actually managed the property in case of any problems. Others contained two or three sheets of again poorly photocopied paper, which were a little better, but contained very limited information other than the address of the property and a string of do's and don'ts.

My view is that it is all about the professional image and high quality of service that you provide to customers. By supplying poorly thought out, and very poor quality documents, which contain little or no information, this will not create the right image or do anything at all for customer confidence.

I spent considerable time gathering information that would be useful to guests and compiling all of it into a user friendly, easy to read guide. There were a number of reasons why I did this, the main being that I wanted to create the right impression, make customer holidays stress free, provide them with plenty of information about the property they would be staying in and then cover, in some detail, areas such as leisure, recreation, dining and places of interest.

I included detailed directions and provided good quality maps on which I highlighted the route to be taken from the airport that they would be arriving at in Florida to whichever property they would be staying at.

I have included a brief list of headings below, which I included in my Customer Information Packs and it has to be said that I received countless positive comments about it from so many people. Again, as a side issue, I even went on to generate money from that idea as well by producing and selling detailed information packs to other villa or property owners, which they then used for their customers.

Those headings included:

1. Travelling to America:
   This included information in relation to arrival at the airport, Passport Control, Immigration and Customs – all of which was intended to make the guests arrival as smooth and trouble free as possible.
2. Vehicle Rental:
   This provided re-assuring information about exactly where the vehicle rental company desks were located, the location of the rental car collection / return area, the types of vehicle available, the standard of those vehicles, information in relation to automatic transmission and the do's and don'ts of driving in America!
3. Directions from the airport to the villa:
   In addition to the detailed written directions, I always included a detailed, easy to navigate road map. The map was divided into three sections i.e.
   a) An overview of the state of Florida so that guests could see the general area, cities and airports.

b) A road map with the roads highlighted in a very bright colour so that the guest could follow the directions given and relate it on the map in front of them.

c) A detailed street map of exactly where the villa was located i.e. within an estate / community etc.

All of the above were very easy to read and follow. This prevented guests from becoming lost, kept blood pressure at the right level and got the guests holiday off to the right start, especially after a long flight!

4. Introduction to the Villa / Property: - (including)

a) The full address of the villa, including zip / post code, and villa telephone number.

b) Key collection instructions (i.e. villa 'wall mounted key lock box' code(s) or directions to where the villa keys could be collected.

c) Any entrance gate key codes (normally for gated communities) that may be required.

d) If the property had a safe or lock box for the use of clients, any key or access code.

e) Full details of the Property Management Company or Property Managers, including the name & office address, daytime and 'out of hours' emergency telephone numbers. These details are required in the event that the client should encounter any problem whilst staying at the villa.

f) Details in relation to the do's and don'ts of the air conditioning. (This prevented unnecessary damage being caused to the system and helped keep utility bills to the minimum!)

g) Details of waste disposal / collection etc.

h) Swimming Pool / Pool deck safety rules and warnings!

5. Visitor Local Information:

This generally covered the estate, community or area where the villa was located and included play parks for children, communal facilities (such as swimming pool, any club house or sports facilities / tennis / volley ball courts etc.).

I also included a section in relation to golf courses, as there are thousands in Florida to choose from.

6. <u>Tourist Attractions:</u>

This was quite a detailed section, and as it was Florida, there was so much to include in relation to theme parks, places of scientific interest, beaches, wildlife, sporting activities, the list could have gone on and on, but I gave a brief overview of each attraction which would be enough to satisfy the interest of most guests.

7. <u>Restaurants - Dining out / Eating-In:</u>

This was a particular subject which was close to my heart as I enjoy good food and good places to eat out. As it happened, this was also one of the most highly publicised and advertised 'pass times' in America, where food is simply in absolute abundance. You may recall that earlier I spoke about how food was advertised everywhere you looked or listened! In America I found that it was virtually impossible to escape the claws of food marketing. A guide to good food and good service highlighted what I thought were the best restaurants and enabled my guests to avoid the poor or mediocre places.

8. <u>Local Currency / Banking:</u>

This section provided basic information and a currency converter for easy and immediate reference, which according to many guests, was ideal when out shopping for the first time in America. I also included information and directions to local banks or ATM's which could be of real use to guests.

9. <u>Shopping outlets In Florida:</u>

This subject was again of great interest to many people, especially those who had never visited Florida before and had little knowledge or experience of the vast amount of shopping malls and designer label or electrical outlets that were available. Included within that were quick reference conversion charts in relation to clothing and shoe sizes and made the essential comparison between the UK and the US for when those essential bargain buys came along!

10. <u>Departure Information:</u>

As every holiday has to end sometime, this section covered leaving the villa and departing for the airport. It included the important issues of what to do with the keys and how long it would take to travel to the airport. This was particularly useful for guests, and it ensured that they left in sufficient time to prevent missing a flight, allowing them enough time to return their hire vehicle, but did not arrive too early where they would just spend hours sitting about an airport.

As part of the information pack that I provided to guests, I also included maps and discount vouchers, which provided great savings, especially for families when eating out. You may recall that I had previously mentioned these vouchers when I had first arrived in Florida and that they are an accepted way of life. These voucher booklets were free and could be found in abundance at the road side and especially near shopping malls and restaurants.

Every time I travelled to Florida I would come back with piles of free tourist maps, discount voucher booklets and free visitor guides in relation to such attractions as Walt Disney-World, Universal Studios, SeaWorld and NASA to name but a few, all of which were used to enhance my guest information pack. These were the little touches that cost me nothing but ensured great feedback from guests.

All in all, the information that I provided in a professional, colourful format, ensured that guests had sufficient information to allow them to plan their holiday and at the same time, create a very high state of excitement while doing so!

In addition, the care that I had taken in compiling and supplying information to guests ensured that customer's had everything that they needed, especially if they had never been in that particular country before and prevented any unnecessary worries or concerns that otherwise they may have had.

Going that extra mile for my guests certainly paid off!

Just by way of a side issue, you will recall that when I had been in the town of Celebration using the telephone, I had also mentioned that I had thought of another opportunity to generate income. As I had outlined in my customer information pack, the villa's all had telephones and guests would certainly use them to telephone friends or family whilst they were in Florida. That created the opportunity for me to sell telephone cards to guests, which I certainly did!

Not everyone's mobile telephone worked whilst in America or if it did, the cost of international telephone calls could be astronomical. Therefore, they would probably use a landline telephone somewhere, whether it be located in the villa or a public telephone. Again, it would probably cost a considerable amount of money if they used a credit card to pay for calls so therefore, after some research a supplier was found where telephone cards could be bought over the internet and sold to guests, again at a profit. The cards provided approximately six hours of talk time, landline to landline – or obviously less if it was to a mobile telephone, and I found that the price, which included a healthy profit margin, was just right and they sold very well indeed. Another good service to customers, which saved them money and generated easy additional income.

It was all about providing good, professional service to customers and making sure that when you received an enquiry that you hung onto it. I had spoken with so many property owners over the years, and so many of them could not understand how they were losing those enquiries and failing to convert them into hard cash.

To me, it was obvious! So many of those owners may have been doing everything right whilst speaking with potential guests, right up to the point when the topic of flights was raised or discussed. That's where the problem really started.

Instead of property owners researching the issue and identifying where they could 'safely' refer guests for flights, whilst still making sure that they would confirm the booking into their property, by failing to do so, that turned a potential booking into absolutely nothing.

It was so obvious that when potential guests were looking for flights, that any travel agent would probably also try and generate more income by teasing custom away from private villa owners by attempting to supply all of the package themselves. Putting it simply, they did it because that's why they are in business, to offer a full range of services and to make money!

I had taken a good look at this problem and thought of various ways of trying to deal with it, however, without an ABTA or ATOL bond it was going to be a difficult problem for me to deal with personally as I could not provide that service. The only thing that I could do in the short to medium term was to approach a travel agent and negotiate some kind of deal where I could make sure that if my customers required flights, that the travel agent would supply the service and not attempt to tease the customer away from me. It was a risk and I was aware of the possibility of that happening, however, I had little choice in the matter.

Once again, I researched the problem and potential solution and then identified the person whom I needed to speak with and who could possibly assist me. As it turned out, it was a great success and due to the business relationship that developed with a very good high street travel agent, I was able to ensure that customers could book flights at very competitive prices, from which I would also receive a commission, and more importantly, ensure that I did not lose any villa bookings to anyone else.

This also applied to the supply of vehicle hire, theme park and attraction tickets and travel insurance. Many of my customers required many, if not all, of these services and that was another way that even more income could be generated.

You will recall that I mentioned the issue of vehicle hire earlier and how the process worked, especially in relation to booking, paying and collecting a hire vehicle. The only thing to add at this point is the fact that so many property owners shy away from supplying this, and many other services, such as theme park and attraction tickets etc. simply because they either do not realise that they can make money out of such products or they do not have the self confidence to research and supply the products themselves or via a supplier who will pay them a commission.

It is not difficult to make money from all of these additional services and the whole process is not at all complicated.

There are many reputable suppliers out there, no matter where your property may be, and all of those companies will want to increase their annual turnover and profit margins. All you need is the confidence to contact such suppliers and negotiate what services they can offer to you for the benefit of your customers, how the process will work and how much you will receive for doing so.

This is an easy way of increasing your overall turnover and, more importantly, increasing your profit margins, whilst making sure that your customers stay with you. It's also another great way of ensuring that your customers will receive a first class service from you.

Everything that you do should be geared toward giving the customer exactly what they want, in a timely and professional manner, which will help ensure that the customer will come back to you year after year, and very importantly, spread the good word!

Always remember, never be afraid to ask for discount or net prices on anything and everything that you need, and that applies to these additional services as well. Don't forget that there is always a deal available from someone. If you can't get it from one – go to another until you get what you want at a price that you are prepared to pay. What's the worst that can happen if you are trying to get discount? All someone can say is no and then just move on to someone that will say yes and are prepared to do business with you. Remember the discounts and reductions in costs that I mentioned earlier when I bought my property abroad, well this is all part of the same overall principle. Everything that you do should either keep money in your pocket or generate more income to put money back into your pocket.

As you will have clearly worked out by now, marketing and advertising your holiday property and the additional services that you can offer to customers is absolutely essential. Once you have all of your administrative systems in place, including your critical diary process so that nothing is missed or forgotten, try and identify the best times to advertise. This may be seasonal depending upon where your property is located.

As my property was in Florida, I found that it was always in demand, but customer demand in comparison with times of the year for effective advertising did actually differ.

An example of such is that there are certain times of the year which, as previously mentioned, if it were possible I could have sold over and over again. There were also different times of the year when advertising yielded a more effective and more positive response than other times of the year.

I always found that the two best times of the year for advertising were firstly, just after the festive period, when people had just got through the Christmas and New Year period and they needed to look forward to a holiday. That also coincided with the abundance of adverts on the television and radio from travel agents advertising holidays all over the world. Secondly, when the summer school holidays were over and people had just returned from a fabulous time in the sun, many looked toward their holiday for the following year. Both were great times to get the adverts out there and show people what you had to offer, again, at a great price that would catch the eye of your potential audience.

As part of the advertising strategy, I had already distributed newsletters by both e-mail and by post, to customers and anyone else that I could think of. The newsletters were not just personally addressed to the recipient, which made them feel special, but the balance in relation to the information content and the colourful presentation was deliberately designed to ensure that the attention of the recipient was immediately drawn and held long enough to get them interested.

That whole process was repeated on a regular basis and it was remarkable how successful it was. I firmly believe that it was due to a mixture of customers actually experiencing a holiday booked with myself and the attention to detail that was taken to ensure that they had a great time, combined with the repeated and regular contact with them, which put my name before anyone else in their mind.

You will soon see how the number of newsletters will steadily grow as your business develops and the financial return from this particular element of targeted advertising becomes more and more successful.

As a side issue, as time goes by and you become more and more confident with your newsletters, keep copies of each one you send out and after a while look back and see how much you will have developed in terms of content, quality and design. That is a good measure of how you are progressing as your business grows and brings with it new ideas.

The last thing I would like to add before I summarise my own secrets to success is an issue of how to keep financial control of your property and ultimately, your destiny.

I have spoken with many people over the years who either own or have owned property abroad and one of the things that really stands out and that alarms me so much is the way that many property owners seem to trust others, whom they do not know, with issues in relation to their personal finances.

Examples of this include where property owners put trust in others to pay for things on their behalf such as their mortgage payments or utility bills, which if not careful, could lead to serious problems and financial disaster for the owner if the payments are not made on time, or worse still, not made at all. That can lead to gas, electric or water supplies being cut off, TV or telephone lines being disconnected or worst of all, the property being foreclosed upon. How do you explain that to guests who are either at the property when it happens or arrive to find that they can not gain access to the home?

Basically, my view is that I would never trust anyone else with my personal financial affairs. In this day and age, when personal banking and utility payments can be set up and dealt with so easily via internet banking, why on earth leave things to someone else, when you can deal with these issues yourself and have the peace of mind that firstly, you are in control and secondly, bills are being paid and on time.

So, in a nutshell, the following is a summary of my 'Top 40 Secrets to Success'. They have worked for me and generated a considerable sum of money so why should they not work for you?

1. If you need or want to generate income from your holiday home, treat your property as a small business.
2. Prepare a simple business plan – don't make it too complicated and do not spend forever doing it, otherwise you will do nothing else.
3. Listen to someone who knows the market, knows what they are doing and knows what they are talking about!
4. Be organised – have your administrative systems in place and everything at your finger tips. If you are chaotic that's how you will sound and appear to customers.
5. Keep a back up copy of all your records. Even though your systems may be held on computer, make sure that you regularly back up those records and keep original copies of any paper based correspondence just in case!
6. Get a good web site with high quality attractive images of your property and e-mail facility for immediate and direct access by customers. Carefully consider and identify a suitable and appropriate e-mail address! Remember, this needs to portray your professional image.
7. Use good quality stationary / letterheads / logos etc. – it looks professional, portrays the right image to reassure and gains the trust and confidence of customers.
8. Advertising is the life blood of your business and it should be a permanent and constantly ongoing activity.

9. Identify as many places as possible that will allow you to advertise free of charge.

10. Try to target your audience – these are the people who have either been to your property or to the area where it is located or who have expressed an interest in doing so. This prevents the 'shotgun blast' approach, which is not very scientific and may not reap the rewards that you expect. It will also help keep advertising costs to the absolute minimum.

11. Be contactable – make sure that you have both a landline (home) telephone number and a mobile telephone number included in all of your advertising. If you are not at home, ensure that you have either diverted your landline to your mobile in order that you can immediately respond to an enquiry, or if that is not possible, have the answering machine or voice mail facility activated with a warm and welcoming message for your customers. Do not forget to include your e-mail address, which is incredibly important as you may find that you receive a vast amount of your enquiries from potential guests via e-mail.

12. If a customer contacts you, DO NOT DELAY in either speaking with them or acknowledging their e-mail enquiry. No matter what you are doing or how tired you are, speak or make contact with them straight away and get the information to them immediately. If you don't, they will go elsewhere and you will be the one who loses out. Remember, if you live in what could be described as a 'busy household', be aware of any distractions and background noise which may put the customer off or make you sound or appear unprofessional.

13. If you agree a time, day and date to re-contact the customer, do not let them down. Log it in your diary so that you do not forget. This applies to any kind of contact, including meetings etc. The over riding factors are to be reliable and be punctual. This approach will pay dividends!

14. Consider everyone to be an opportunity for business and ultimately a way of putting money into your pocket.

Whoever you speak with, let them know about your business and what you can do for them.

15. Know and understand your product and how each element works. Get to know the area and guest facilities in relation to where your property is located i.e. on the estate or community as your personal knowledge will really appeal to your customers. This will also assist in your sales pitch.

16. Get to know local tourist attractions – go there and visit, gain first hand personal experience, its all part of your market research!

17. Rehearse what you are going to say and how you are going to say it. If you can, sell the idea of what you do and what you supply in the first sentence as this will immediately help to secure the customers interest.

18. Be confident and portray that confidence when speaking with customers.

19. Be professional, warm, friendly and courteous when speaking with customers.

20. Get excited and be enthusiastic about your business when talking with customers. That is something that really rubs off onto them and is a great tool to turn an enquiry into a confirmed booking, and ultimately, hard cash!

21. Give customers your undivided attention and a very personal service tailored to meet their needs, requirements and expectations.

22. Make your customers feel special and don't forget - **YOU WANT SOMEONE TO BUY SOMETHING FROM YOU!** Be positive, be motivated and let people hear that in your voice!

23. Obtain the details i.e. name, postal address, e-mail address and telephone number(s) of all customers for future advertising purposes.

24. If a customer does not get back to you within a few days, you have their contact details, so do a follow up call –don't be afraid, it really does work!

25. Do not get disheartened if customers do not book with you

straight away – keep going, the cheques will fall through the letter box onto the carpet.

26. Be flexible – be prepared to accept a little less if it is a small number in the party. As they say – less is more! Be competitive and be prepared to adjust your prices for smaller numbers of guests as your overheads will be less and customers will book with you as they will be very happy indeed that they have got a good deal and a reduction in price. Very importantly, they will also 'spread the word' and come back to you in the future!

27. If you have a good stream of advertising, one where you are getting great returns, good results and actually generating income from, keep it to yourself, don't kill the golden goose! If you start telling other property owners, they will also try and tap into the 'golden stream' and that will undoubtedly create competition and you could well lose out to other property owners.

28. Look to supply other services, such as vehicle hire, theme park & attraction tickets, telephone cards and flights. Initially this will be via other sources in return for them helping you – commission based of course! Also remember, flights and all of the other services that I have mentioned, could be to any destination in the world and not just where your property is located. Do not limit yourself, open up your business by opening up your mind and supply customers with what they want!

29. Give your customers something for nothing! It does not have to be large or expensive, after all, you are in business to make money and you are not a charity. I have mentioned items such as a telephone card or small food packs for when guests arrive at your property. Relatively small and inexpensive items, but they will go a long way to making your customers very happy indeed and they will remember you for it as well!

30. Give your customers good information packs. That includes when they first make contact with you, in the form

of a 'brochure', and also after they confirm the booking with you. Items such as maps, discount vouchers, and information about local tourist attractions go down very well indeed with customers.

31. Newsletters – to previous customers / enquirers really work! This is a great way to ensure regular contact in order to remind people that you are still there and providing a great service. The newsletters should always be professional, and in my view, at least monthly. They should be informative, balanced, show the services that you can supply and any discounts that you may have available as an incentive for customers to book with you. Show customers why you are different to the rest!

32. Do not turn anyone away! If you have an enquiry from a customer which you can not accommodate because your property is booked for the dates they require, never turn them away or let them go! Form an alliance with other property owners where you can assist the customer and not disappoint them. Generate business for other holiday home owners, but build in a handling / referral fee to generate more income for yourself. This will also work in reverse so that other property owners can assist you to generate income.

33. Never be afraid to knock on someone's door. If you need help with something, whatever it may be, never be afraid to research it and go out and find the person that can help you develop your business. You have nothing to lose and everything to gain!

34. Networking opens doors! Do not be afraid to speak with other property owners and those who are in a similar business to yourself. Look for opportunities to meet with people 'in the trade' either through local travel companies or through business seminars or locally organised small business meetings.

35. 'Piggybacking' is a great way of growing your business while keeping your overheads and general costs down to

the absolute minimum. Look for ways of developing business alliances where larger travel companies are keen to use and sell your product, but very importantly, use their money to indirectly advertise your business to their customers!

36. When you think of a good idea to improve your business, write it down straight away. If you don't, you'll forget and that may cost you money.

37. Do not put things off! If you do, something else will come along which you deem to be more important and you will end up missing things, which in turn will make you unreliable and give you a poor reputation. Deal with things straight away and this approach will prevent you from putting yourself, and your business, under pressure.

38. At the end of every day, review what you have achieved today and what your plan is for tomorrow. Be structured – be coordinated – be realistic!

39. Constantly remind yourself of all the positive things you have achieved. Set targets and timescales and reward yourself in some way when you achieve those milestones.

40. Last, but not least, if you are not confident about dealing with tax returns or are unsure about what you may be able to claim or offset against your business etc., employ the services of an accountant as this may keep money in your pocket and ensure that you keep timely and accurate records!

Business, to me, is all about making money! If you think that way, and you consider my 'Top 40 Tips' you will have everything in place to give you the very best start on your road to success.

CHAPTER 9

Minding Your Own Business

When I look back at how and why I entered into such a venture and all of the ground work that I did to make sure that I had solid foundations on which to build my business, I sometimes have to pinch myself to just check that what I achieved was real.

As I have indicated, I was always looking for ways to improve and develop both my business and myself and some of my ideas really bore fruit. After a while, it became clear to me that some people appeared irritated by my progression. Some individuals that I came across had been involved in property abroad for a little longer than me, and it appeared that they were desperately trying, for whatever reason, to control others who were less experienced.

Some of those characters were critical of my innovative style and because of the negativity or jealousy that they displayed toward me, I very coldly and clinically cut them out of my life.

My business prospered, and it would appear, that theirs did not - C'est la vie!

Be careful not to associate or take advice from negative people.

I decided that I would be very careful indeed with whom I would either take into my confidence or do business with as I could not allow anything to impede or distract me from achieving my goal.

In pursuit of my ambition for a complete change in lifestyle, I managed to carve the foundations of my dream through sheer determination and hard work.

By the very nature of some of the characters that I knew or had worked with over many years, I was bound to meet cynicism along the way. Some people and close friends were quite complimentary and supportive of what I was doing, however, others were quite narrow minded and could not see the rut that they were in, but I suppose that is just life. Some were stuck in that vicious cycle of working to pay the never ending bills, and some thought it was great if they worked even longer hours on overtime to get a few more pounds. Maybe they could not see a way out from that, maybe they were resigned to that way of life, or maybe they were just happy.

Something that really did bug me was that some colleagues or associates seemed to do anything and everything that they could to put anyone down who did not conform to the stereotype drone. Anyone trying to better themselves in any way should be admired, however, some people can not help themselves and they just have to say something derogatory. Jealousy plays a big part in some people and the sweet smell of success can make others green with envy. It became obvious to me that the more successful I became, the more some tried to discredit me, my excellent business reputation and growing success.

I rose above that and the bottom line is don't let anyone effect what you are trying to achieve. Just ride it out and inwardly laugh at those who mock or have a go at you as you take money out of their pockets and put it in yours. My view is that people like that are narrow minded and are going no where fast. They might think that they have a good job or even a decent income, but they are limiting themselves in life. They are in a vicious circle and maybe find it so difficult to escape from it that they have just given up and rolled over.

You may recall that I had devised a system to help both myself and other property owners. I was quite pleased with my idea of the Customer Referral System and it actually showed my willingness to help others.

Money can be a powerful, yet strange elixir at times. On occasions it clouds people's judgement and can cause some to show their true colours. If you do not keep your own council, things can become difficult. In my experience, some people turn and change as greed overcomes them. Unfortunately, some are so intellectually moribund that they can not see the bigger picture – they think of today and not tomorrow, next month, next year or beyond.

One of the other things that you may experience is that so many people will have a go and offer there 'considered and expert views' on something that they know absolutely sod all about.

You may have to overcome this, some laughed, some had a go at me as I tried to better myself, but my question to them was, "What have you done over the last ten years to progress or give yourself some kind of personal satisfaction, or life changing experience? If the answer is nothing or if you have nothing constructive to say – then don't say it.

As always in my daytime job, I absolutely admired people who got things done, and who possessed vision, foresight, drive and determination. That view also spread to the world of business, and in particular, to those who were self made and very successful. However, for those who have done nothing for themselves and can only criticise or try to belittle others, deal with them firmly. These are the very people who you will be able to laugh all the way to the bank about, and probably with some of their money in your pocket to boot!

CHAPTER 10

Enjoying the dream –
Growing the Business

It has to be said that owning a holiday home abroad is quite a fantastic experience. The thought alone actually makes you feel good, the reality of it being even better providing of course that everything is going to plan, you are satisfied with what you have and how it is being looked after in your absence.

If you are one of those people who are completely satisfied with your property abroad, you will know exactly what I mean.

I can not think of a better feeling of personal satisfaction when you open the front door of your holiday home in the sun, walk through the house, open the patio doors and dive straight into your own private swimming pool. You may want to stop just for a second and ditch your valuables before you jump in!

I look back over the years to when I first had the dream of buying property abroad and what has happened since. I often have to stop and take stock of what I have achieved and how my life, and the way that I now think, has actually changed.

After starting off with a dream, combined with total commitment and an abundance of determination, I have now moved on to bigger and better things.

As a direct result of how I approached this business venture, it soon became apparent to me that there were some great opportunities to be seized which would certainly grow the business and produce the rewards that I was looking for.

As a result of being successful at marketing the property that I owned abroad and generating the maximum income possible from one home, I soon formed a partnership with a friend who owned similar property in the same area to where my property was located. The result of this partnership soon produced some very good ideas and after initially formulating a business plan 'on the back of a beer mat', we started off on a journey which would see us developing a business which would soon start to generate considerable turn over!

We knew that we had some good ideas in relation to the services that customers would either need or require when looking to buy a holiday and we also had the confidence to seek out ways of supplying those services at very competitive prices. We also knew that it was essential to combine those services with the personal touch that every customer expects and deserves.

We looked at every aspect and soon started to draw up the list of services that we could directly offer or indirectly supply, which included flights, private holiday villa's, vehicle hire, travel insurance, theme park and attraction tickets and even telephone cards.

In order to provide those services we went through the process of firstly, actually finding a way of supplying all of the above and secondly, having a new company web site designed to promote and sell them. The web site on its own was a mine field. We soon got our eyes opened in relation to issues such as intellectual property rights, design and production costs and how some designers offered all kinds of eye catching gimmicks to us in relation to web site design, but when it boiled down to it, they did not have the expertise or the artistic flair that would set our web site in a class of its own. Nor could they secure the hits to the web site via the internet search engines that we were looking for.

The costs that some were demanding were just unreal and we certainly had to be realistic and walk before we could run. To cut a long story very short, we eventually had a web site designed which included an associated e-mail facility. This, I have to say, was not the best web site in the world but it was certainly good enough to show all the services that we could supply and it got us up, running and making money.

It was not long before our advertising started to produce results and the enquiries started to pour in. As part of the business plan, and to compliment the web site, we worked hard to attract other property owners who were interested in doing business with us and who were more than willing to allow us to place our guests into there holiday property. As part of our web site, there was a facility where we could illustrate some of the holiday homes that were now registered with our company and this provided very attractive images of detached holiday homes in Florida, with their own private swimming pools, which could be browsed at leisure by potential guests.

We had a very simple layout, which was very easy on the eye, and extremely easy to navigate too. We could show with ease what we had on offer and the associated prices and availability.

This allowed me to speak with customers and whilst on the telephone guide them through the site, and ultimately turn enquiries into confirmed bookings very quickly.

You will remember me saying earlier that you should never be afraid to knock on someone's door if you think that they can help you develop your business, well that's exactly what we had to do on many occasions. We wanted to supply other services, but as we were just two people with what we thought were some good ideas, we somehow had to get the backing of major companies or suppliers to enable us to buy in the services at a good price to sell out at a reasonable profit.

As a result of approaching many suppliers, and after being rejected by quite a few I have to add, through perseverance and self belief in what we were doing, arrangements were very quickly put in place to enable us to supply vehicle hire, theme park tickets, travel insurance and even the telephone cards that I mentioned earlier. The two big things that had a dramatic effect on the business were firstly, the ability to supply flights and secondly, take credit / debit card payments for any of the services we wanted to sell. Taking immediate payment was the one thing that would bug us for a while and as such, in the early days we had to rely on cheque's or cash. Waiting for cheques obviously took time and the vast amount of customers actually wanted to pay by some form of plastic card in any event.

The issue in relation to not being able to supply flights that we encountered in those early days meant that although we were providing a great service in relation to villa accommodation, vehicle hire and the other services that we had available, we were losing customers at the point where they were trying to book their flights.

Somehow we had to stop that as it was costing us considerable amounts of money and we were losing custom. As a result, we had no alternative but to do some networking, knock on doors and find out which of the high street travel agents would work with us and actually back us.

After much thought and several meetings, we managed to secure an arrangement with a very large independent high street travel agent who was prepared to do business with us. As a result, this not only allowed us to supply commissioned based flights and some other services through them, but this give us the facility to expand rapidly and move into the whole wide world of travel!

When I say the whole world, that's exactly what I mean. We had started off with our two holiday homes in Florida, but after looking closely at what we thought we could offer, we turned those thoughts into reality and started advertising and selling every type of holiday that you could think of, in any part of the world, at very competitive prices.

As far as we were concerned, there wasn't a thing that we could not offer to our customers. All that we had to do was make sure that our advertising was right and that it actually screamed out that we were not just about Florida, and that whatever they needed, in any part of the world, we could deliver at outstanding prices.

We spent a considerable amount of time getting our advertising right and getting the word out that we had now gone worldwide, but we never forgot that Florida was and always would be a massive part of the business.

In a very short space of time we had become successful on the smaller scale as property owners, then as a result of vision and hard work, we were now branching out and supplying any service that we could get our hands on to ensure that we had happy customers who were saving money, who would spread the word and come back to us year after year.

This was undoubtedly a major break through for us and we found ourselves in a position where we had many property owners who were coming to us looking to do business.

As a result, we became stronger in the world of business both as individuals and as a company, and we made sure that even though we were growing the business, we would never forget the essential elements of treating both property owners and our customers with the utmost respect whilst providing a very personal service to meet their needs. In effect we took all of the hard work away from them and that, I have to say, paid dividends. The property owners were receiving very reasonable rates of payment from us indeed for allowing us to use their property for our guests, and our customers were getting fantastic holidays in exceptionally good quality accommodation. This, in turn, helped to make sure that when they came to us, they would get the holiday of a lifetime. We also took care of the paperwork in relation to the customers on behalf of the villa owners and this proved to be a very good all round package indeed.

In no time at all, we had developed our business plan and expanded the company to include the following services:-

European and Worldwide Holidays

- Florida Specialists
- Package Holidays
- City Breaks

190

- Specialist Holidays
- Cruises
- Safaris
- Skiing Holidays
- Wedding Packages
- Escorted Holidays and Excursions
- Lapland - Christmas Specials

Flights and Accommodation

- European and Worldwide Flights
- Private Villas
- Hotels

Car Hire

- European and Worldwide Car Hire

Holiday Extras

- Theme Park and Attraction Tickets
- Travel Insurance
- Airport Hotels
- Airport Transfers
- Airport Car Parking
- UK Airport Private Lounges
- Foreign Currency Exchange
- Telephone Cards

One thing that never changed was the very simple fact that whether we had one villa or a thousand villas and were offering all kinds of different services, we knew that the life blood of the company would be down to our advertising strategy. We had to make certain that we made contact, on a continuous basis, with as many people as possible, and in turn, get those customers to spend their money with us.

This undoubtedly worked and our turn over grew rapidly, way beyond our wildest dreams. The only initial problem that we encountered was making sure that people knew that we were not just selling holidays to Florida, but we were now supplying anything and everything that a customer could ever want. The world was now truly our oyster!

I have mentioned advertising constantly throughout, and once again I make no apologies whatsoever about that fact, as without that, your business is going to go down the pan. I have talked about the detail of how and what I have found to be successful advertising, but I will now mention two things that I found as we grew.

The first is that generating income at whatever level, whether it is as a lone property owner or a larger company, is so important to make sure that you realise your dream and remain afloat! The problem is that other people who may be in a position to help you may not see that as a priority for themselves. Unless you do something positive about that, you are in the hands of the gods!

The people whom you are relying upon to help you get your name known out there and facilitate your advertising in order to generate income, often become busy with something else and forget or decide that they will do something for you next week, which turns into never, as something else will come along to distract them. They do not realise what it means or just how important it is to you and your business venture.

You need to find a way of building a good rapport with those people and do it in a way which is positive for you whilst not appearing to be either placing others under pressure or badgering them into doing what you have asked of them. If you go about it the wrong way, you will not achieve your aim. It is different of course if you have paid for a service and you are not receiving what you have agreed and paid them to do. In that case, its game on and ensure that you get everything that you have agreed to, and maybe more as a result of being inconvenienced!

I found that as a result of regular contact with the people that I approached to assist me, it was possible to make sure that regular advertising to the same target audiences was achieved.

The beauty of this is the more you target an audience, the more they will see your name and the more people will subconsciously think about you when they are looking to buy a holiday or other product. Don't forget, think of the most cost effective way of doing this and ideally where you are allowed to advertise your services free of charge.

The result being, careful targeting – free of charge, puts more money in your pocket!

The second issue is one of trying to assist others, and when I say others, I mean other property owners. There were many times that we would have so many guests who had booked and paid for holidays in private villas that we simply ran out of the 'stock' that we had registered with our company and we had to find and 'buy in' more properties. I have spoken with so many property owners and I have to say that I have had the pleasure of speaking with some very nice people, and alternatively, some very arrogant people and some who, putting it mildly, just have not got a clue about business or how to operate their dream home in such a way that it actually generates income for them.

So many people were disbelieving when I first spoke with them and to give them the benefit of the doubt, in relation to some, I understood their point of view. When I first told them about our company, what we did and how we did it, many had concerns about it, however once they overcame their initial reservations and took that chance of working with us, they thought that we were a dream come true!

I have no doubt that we saved a number of property owners from going under as a result of placing guest bookings with them, which in turn, generated sufficient income for them to stay afloat.

I always had an open mind whenever I spoke with a property owner for the first time, but with some, it was clear that there was simply nothing that I could do for them. That was normally due to their attitude and inflexibility. I used to spend time trawling through web sites where various types of property were being advertised for short term rental, and where owners had paid considerable amounts of money for the privilege to advertise their home. When I researched what was available, it was clear that due to the amounts of money being requested by some owners that they were asking way over the odds and were pricing themselves out of the market. Some others were virtually giving their property away just to entice custom. That to me also sounded the alarm that maybe those owners were in trouble and that they would possibly welcome help from other sources.

With some, how wrong could I have been? As mentioned, it was clear that when I spoke with them that they had a real attitude problem and they cast doubt upon our business, our integrity, and for that matter, us in general. In the end, I would just end the conversation by saying that I did not think that we could do business with them and wished them well for the future. A vast majority of those people were 'new to the game' and they were telling me how to run a business of this nature. I have also lost count of the number of property owners who gave me a hard time and cast doubt on us and later made contact asking for our assistance. Some, I have to say we helped, however with others, due to their whole attitude of still trying to tell us what to do and how to do it, we just cast them to the wind. Maybe one day they might reflect upon their folly, who knows?

You can now see that if you have vision and drive that virtually anything is possible.

One thing that I learned is that team dynamics can be very different and individuals whom have certain qualities can be priceless!

Examples of these dynamics can soon become apparent when you go into business in whatever form it may be. These may range from dominant partners when, for example, two couples may have jointly purchased a property to let or it might be apparent in the individual skills that people may possess.

I have to say that with my business partner and I, the dynamics were very clear indeed. We often discussed how our different qualities actually assisted the growth of the business.

I found that I was very comfortable contacting and speaking with people, whether it be on the telephone or in person, arranging meetings, and organising effective, timely and fail safe administrative systems whereas my partner was better at other tasks.

Alternatively, when I first started in that business I was aware that my weak point, or area for development as they say, was clearly in relation to my IT skills. I was absolutely appalling with computers and I used to become very frustrated when it came to using them, especially if I was on a tight time line and I could not get the bloody thing to do what I wanted.

I also seemed to have this aura around me that ensured that whenever I went anywhere near any type of IT system, or even a printer for that matter, the thing would crash, adding to my stress levels!

As time went by, and after being given guidance on many occasions, I became more familiar and confident with computer systems and programmes. I took basic IT in my stride and overcame many problems and challenges that I encountered.

We also became good at producing things such as newsletters and advertising flyers on the computer systems and over time, we could actually see how we were making progress as the quality of our literature improved every time that we produced something.

I think its amazing how things progressed and with it I noticed that the opinions, views and comments of some also changed as the business grew. In the early days we used to get the sarcastic comments and jibes about being wannabee businessmen. As our good reputation grew, they became respectful queries and questions in relation to holidays and our business in general. Some of the very people who tried to put us down actually came to us in the end and put money into our pockets. Personally, I think that spoke volumes about us, about our business and about our reputation for providing excellent service and value for money!

I found that what we achieved had been very time consuming and hard work, however, it has also been very rewarding and satisfying to say the least. I have not been one for going out every night on the drink and instead, I have channeled my time, energy, drive and vision into something which I, and my family, will hopefully benefit from in the long term.

More importantly, as we have a little girl, I am doing this to give her the very best chance and start in life as possible. You never know, she may want to go into business herself one day and what I am doing now may assist her to carve out her future aspirations, dreams and desires!

Chapter 11

Reflections

I have always been the type of person who never trusts in good luck alone to enable me to achieve my goals in life. To me, there is no substitute for hard work, commitment and the sheer determination to succeed, even when you think that the odds may be stacked against you. The thought of the challenge in itself is always enough for me to hit it head on and grind out the result that I am looking for, whatever that may relate to at that particular time. All that I do is remain totally focused on the rewards that wait when the job is complete.

The principles of what I have outlined in this book, combined with my mindset, have been no different at all to the way that I have tackled some of the challenges that I have encountered in my professional 'daytime life' before I entered the world of business. It's just my way of showing myself that I can do anything if I am determined enough.

If I can achieve, then there is absolutely no reason at all why others should not, especially in this particular area of owning and generating income from property abroad. As I pointed out at the very start, this idea is far from unique but the difference is that I have been able to make it work when probably thousands of other property owners have struggled and ended up with very little to show for their initial investment.

I have done my very best to assist others, some of whom have actually appreciated the time and assistance that I have provided. However, it astonishes me that other property owners with whom I have spoken, who are clearly in difficulties both in financial and operating terms, still think that they know best and will not listen to reason or the voice of experience. I suppose with people like that there is only so much that I can do and say before I just tell them that they should continue as they see fit and I then leave them to get on with it. Why should I spend my precious time speaking with people like that when my attention is clearly focussed elsewhere.

There have been some difficult times, but that's just life I guess and when I see money coming in, that makes me forget about the difficulties or the challenges and it actually motivates me to achieve, and earn more.

It's only now that I am clearly starting to see the rewards of my venture and along with it new ideas. If I do have any regrets it's that I should have started my own business years before I actually did, but looking back, I have to say that I was having a great time and my mind was elsewhere.

My focus now is the development and expansion of other business areas and opportunities and I have to say that I am excited about the possibilities that lie ahead. I have gained so much experience and overcome so many challenges that I have no fear for the future and whatever it may bring. Although in relative terms, its only small business, it's my business and what I have achieved, for a person without qualifications and a poor education, actually makes me proud.

As they say, onwards and upwards, let's see what's around the next corner!

Printed in the United Kingdom
by Lightning Source UK Ltd.
134487UK00001B/227/P